Extending Social Research

Extending Social Research

Application, Implementation and Publication

Gayle Letherby and Paul Bywaters

With Zoebia Ali, Paul Allender, Geraldine Brady, Geraldine Brown, Anthea Coghlan, Tony Colombo, Dexter Du Boulay, Maureen Hirsch, Mary Knyspel, Helen Poole, Graham Steventon, Denise Tanner and Corinne Wilson

Open University Press

Open University Press
McGraw-Hill Education
McGraw-Hill House
Shoppenhangers Road
Maidenhead
Berkshire
England
SL6 2QL

email: enquiries@openup.co.uk
world wide web: www.openup.co.uk

and Two Penn Plaza, New York, NY 10121-2289, USA

First published 2007

A catalogue record of this book is available from the British Library

ISBN-10: 0 335 21529 7 (pb)   0 335 21530 0 (hb)
ISBN-13: 978 0 335 21529 4 (pb)   978 0 335 21530 0 (hb)

Library of Congress Cataloguing-in-Publication Data
CIP data applied for

Typeset by RefineCatch Limited, Bungay, Suffolk
Printed in the UK by Bell & Bain Ltd, Glasgow

The **McGraw·Hill** Companies

To John and to Olwen

Contents

     Anthea Coghlan, Gayle Letherby, Denise Tanner, Corinne Wilson
     and Paul Bywaters

     Introduction   90
     Steering groups   92
     Building and maintaining relationships   94
         Access   94
         Methods and methodological experience   95
     Analysis   102
     Commissioner responses   105
     End points   107

7   Outputs   108
     Tony Colombo, Paul Allender, Paul Bywaters and
     Gayle Letherby

     Introduction   108
     Research outputs: what works?   109
     Output strategy and audiences   112
         Target audiences   113
         Managing audience reception   114
         Tailoring outputs to audiences   115
         Enlisting intermediaries   115
     Forms of output   116
         Written outputs   116
         Oral presentations and outputs   118
         Technology and outputs   120
         Media and outputs   121
     End points   122

8   Outcomes   123
     Geraldine Brady, Paul Bywaters, Mary Knyspel,
     Gayle Letherby and Graham Steventon

     Introduction   123
     Arguments against a close relationship between research and
     practice   125
     Key issues   126
     What works?   129
         Young parents: training programme   133
         Young parents: specialist services   136
     Opportunities and barriers   138
     End points   140

Acknowledgements

Although, of course, the responsibility for what we have written remains our own, many people have helped – both directly and indirectly – in the preparation of this book. As overall editors we are grateful to our fellow contributors not only for their written contributions but for their input throughout. Discussions with and comments from our co-authors Zoebia Ali, Paul Allender, Geraldine Brady, Geraldine Brown, Anthea Coghlan, Tony Colombo, Dexter du Boulay, Maureen Hirsch, Mary Knyspel, Helen Poole, Graham Steventon, Denise Tanner and Corinne Wilson have helped us tremendously. Our work and the work of others within and for the Centre for Social Justice (CSJ) at Coventry University has provided the inspiration and support for this book. Without the multi-dimensional help and hard work of Nicola Boyle, as development worker for the Centre, and all of those who have worked on CSJ research and development projects, there would have been much less to write about. Similarly, the collaborative working relationships that we have developed with various research stakeholders have inspired us and helped to shape our thinking. Last, but not least, we are grateful to our editors at Open University Press for their support and patience. Thank you all.

Paul Bywaters and Gayle Letherby

Notes on Contributors

Zoebia Ali is a researcher and lecturer at Coventry University. Zoebia's research interests generally lie in the areas of 'race', disability, childhood and black and minority ethnic health issues. Her PhD explored the perspectives and experiences of Pakistani and Bangladeshi disabled children and young people. She has also been involved in a number of novel and innovative projects at Coventry University's Centre for Social Justice. These include a recently completed health assessment of black and minority ethnic communities in Rugby; young parent research; an ethnicity and young people project, and evaluation of an advocacy service for families of Pakistani and Bangladeshi disabled children.

Paul Allender is a Research Fellow in the Centre for Social Justice, within SURGE (Applied Research Centre in Sustainable Regeneration) at Coventry University. His overall research interests can be summarized under the umbrella of political sociology and specifically the political implications of Foucault's thought. At the Centre for Social Justice, he has undertaken research into hate crime, prisoner resettlement, looked after children and many other topics. He has also done some work which brings artists and social researchers together in collaborative relationships. One of these projects was with Theatre Absolute in Coventry and currently he is working with the Shysters, a theatre company of learning-disabled actors, also in Coventry. He believes that social researchers need to engage with participants *as people*. Any research which treats people as 'subjects' or otherwise as units of measurement is necessarily and inevitably flawed from the outset.

Geraldine Brady is a Research Fellow in the Centre for Social Justice, within SURGE (Applied Research Centre in Sustainable Regeneration) at Coventry University. Her primary research interests are children's perspectives of health and social care and the development of child/young person-inclusive methods; these interests were reflected in her doctoral research, 'Children and Attention Deficit Hyperactivity Disorder (ADHD): a sociological exploration'. Since joining the CSJ in 2004 she has been involved in a number of research projects which have explored the experiences of marginalized or socially excluded groups, in particular young parents and pregnant teenagers.

Geraldine Brown is a Senior Researcher in the Centre for Social Justice, within SURGE (Applied Research Centre in Sustainable Regeneration) at Coventry

University. She has extensive experience of undertaking research for the voluntary, community and academic sectors. Her particular focus has been the extent of social exclusion and the effectiveness of efforts to challenge it. The research she has undertaken has covered a broad range of areas. These include: health and social care policy and practice; the health and social care of teenage parents and black and minority ethnic communities; the health and social care interface; partnership working; community regeneration and housing. A key aim of her work is to promote the voices and views of those who tend to be marginalized.

Paul Bywaters is Emeritus Professor of Social Work at Coventry University and Visiting Professor at the University of Warwick. His central research interests have been in the role social work can play in understanding and combating health inequalities and he initiated and leads the international Social Work and Health Inequalities Network. He also founded the Centre for Social Justice at Coventry University and this has led to involvement in a wide range of applied research activity with a social justice focus, including work on race and disability, older people and emergency department care, 'looked after' children, and self-injury. He is now spending more time with his family and his allotment.

Anthea Coghlan is course leader for a postgraduate programme in public service management, and is a part-time lecturer and research supervisor in social work and psychology at Coventry University. She is a member of a Research Ethics Committee at Unilever. She has an interest in the visual arts and attended a postgraduate course in art history at the Courtauld Institute and a course on psychotherapy and art at Tate Modern. Anthea's research experience includes a resource investigation of an American Airbase, qualitative studies of parenting disabled children and of the impact of New Managerialism. She was also involved in consultancy work in relation to a social justice audit and to institutional racism. Current research interests include social justice in large organizations; alternative models of public service management, and the experiences of Pakistani women of higher education.

Tony Colombo is a Senior Lecturer in the Department of Social and Community Studies, Coventry University, where he teaches and carries out research in a number of areas including work on multi-agency public protection panels; models of mental disorder; prisoner resettlement, and risk and violence. Tony obtained his PhD in criminology from the University of Cambridge through work on multi-agency approaches to the treatment, management and care of mentally disordered offenders. Tony is also the Director of a new research group at Coventry University entitled: The Study and Prevention of Violence and Oppression.

Dexter Du Boulay is a Senior Lecturer in Social Welfare in the Department of

Social and Community Studies, Coventry University. His main research and writing interests are in the mainstreaming of equalities within organizational development; organizational culture within voluntary organizations; capacity building within the black voluntary sector; social housing as social businesses and local community and economic development.

Maureen Hirsch has been a Senior Lecturer in Social Policy at Coventry University. Her main research has been in areas of diversity and equality, including work on asylum and immigration matters and on older people's lives and services. An active interest in how equal opportunities can be put into effect started earlier in her career, when working for the Inner London Education Authority, and has been a continuing theme throughout her working life. Recently she has been involved in critically examining equality issues, around regeneration and community cohesion. Having been elected as a local councillor, she has had the opportunity to engage in the practicalities of trying to put policy into practice.

Mary Knyspel is a Senior Lecturer at Coventry University specializing in research methods and social policy. She has a particular interest in diversity and equal opportunities. Recent research includes work on performance indicators for ethnic monitoring for the Centre for Social Justice on behalf of the City Forum. She has also been involved in research for local health, social services and housing organizations in relation to housing, service satisfaction and quality of life for people receiving mental health care services. Mary has presented at the International Health Promotion Conference and reviewed books for the *Journal of Social Policy* and the *Journal of Sociology of Health and Illness*.

Gayle Letherby is a Professor of Sociology in the School of Law and Social Science at the University of Plymouth. Before moving to Plymouth in October 2005 she was Reader in the Sociology of Gender and Deputy Director of the Centre for Social Justice at Coventry University. Research and writing interests include reproductive and non/parental identities; working and learning in higher education; deviance, crime and criminology, and the sociology of trains and train travel. Throughout her career Gayle has been fascinated and excited by issues of method, methodology and epistemology – including feminist approaches, auto/biography and the relationship between knowing and doing; her involvement in the production of this book is further evidence of this.

Helen Poole is a Senior Lecturer in Criminology at Coventry University. Previous research has included government-funded studies into the use of forensic science in the police investigation process; the DNA Expansion Programme; street crime; arson, and Crime and Disorder Reduction Partnerships. She recently contributed to a study into the housing needs of prisoners with

Coventry University's Centre for Social Justice. She has entries in the *Sage Dictionary of Social Research* and is commencing work on a collaborative book examining issues of surveillance. She is currently researching into education provision in prisons, and has interests in all matters related to punishment. In particular, she is concerned with the impacts of policy on the treatment and status of offenders in general, and especially prisoners.

Graham Steventon is course leader for the undergraduate courses in Criminology and Senior Lecturer at Coventry University. As a qualified architect and urban designer as well as criminologist, his teaching and research interests lie in the interface between crime and its control and the social and spatial environments. His PhD from the University of Warwick explored the nature of informal social control in an affluent community setting and subsequent research with NACRO and the Centre for Social Justice at Coventry University has focused on community safety and crime prevention. He has presented numerous papers in conferences in the UK, America and Canada on his research interests and has published works on spatial research, geographical information systems, designing out crime and defensible space.

Denise Tanner is a Lecturer in Social Work at University of Warwick. Before taking up an academic post, she worked for many years as a social worker and senior social worker, mainly in adult services. Her teaching and research interests include: the well-being of older people; community care policy and practice; the social work role with people experiencing mental distress; and service user involvement. Her doctoral research explored how older people whose needs fell outside social services' eligibility criteria for services managed the difficulties they experienced. She has published work concerned with support services for older people.

Corinne Wilson is a part-time Lecturer in Sociology at Coventry University. She is also a PhD student currently in her writing-up year. Corinne's PhD explores the tensions between prevention and support discourses in relation to teenage pregnancy and young motherhood. She has worked on several research projects at the Centre for Social Justice and her research interests include teenage pregnancy and young motherhood; gender and violence; childhood and surveillance; research method, methodology and epistemology.

Section 1

INTRODUCTION

1

Extending social research

Paul Bywaters and Gayle Letherby

Introduction • Current models of social research • Ending or extending social research? • Authorship and structure • End points

Introduction

What is the purpose of social science research: to understand the world or to change it? In recent years, social science research has been challenged to demonstrate its applicability, its usefulness. As Sandra Nutley argues: 'the current momentum and level of activity associated with the idea of evidence-based policy [or evidence-based practice] is unprecedented, certainly in the UK' (Nutley 2003: 3, our addition). Research councils and funders throughout the world have been increasingly concerned with demonstrating value for money in terms of the applied benefits of social research for economic and social development. For example, the Australian Research Council (2005) claims that it 'plays a key role in the Australian Government's investment in the future prosperity and well-being of the Australian community'. The Canadian Social Science and Humanities Research Council (2005) is currently funding a major research programme on 'Knowledge Impact in Society' and states that its focus is on 'real life' issues. However, curiously, despite these and other motivations for enhancing the impact of social science research on the world it examines and explores, textbook models of the social research process still commonly end at the point when findings are written up, paying little attention to what outputs or outcomes result.

To choose a visual analogy, think of two cliffs with a chasm between them. Hitherto, methodologists have usually written about the end stage of the research process as if researchers stand on one cliff top, holding their findings and passing them around to follow academics. In some cases the findings have been scattered by the wind, landed on the other side and been caught by policy makers, managers and practitioners or by interested lay people and – sometimes – put to use. But in many cases they have been blown by the wind, not reaching the far cliff, and have plummeted to the valley below never to be seen again, or have landed on the same side as the throwers to be read only by other researchers and/or academics. In other cases, only some sheets have reached the other side and messages have been misunderstood, misinterpreted or even deliberately misused. On the first cliff, researchers are heard railing against the failure of the policy makers and practitioners to take them and their findings seriously. In recent times, increasingly sophisticated and expensive mechanisms and institutions for catching, combining, reviewing, analysing and applying findings have been developed on the second cliff (the evidence-based practice 'industry' – see Chapter 2). And the internet has meant that the messages have been much more widely available. But does the gap need to exist in the first place? Can bridges be built between the research community and the application community so that they work alongside each other, with considerations of practice and policy outcomes built into research projects from the start? Can the tasks of research and application be developed as a seamless series of activities (Fox 2003)? And if social science research is not to end when findings have been written up, in what ways does this mean that we have to extend our research models?

Over twenty years ago, Helen Roberts (1984: 199) was complaining about the lack of focus on:

> an aspect of the research process which, although vitally important, tends to be given scant attention in methodology textbooks and courses. This part of the process concerns not the way in which research is funded or carried out ... but the end product of the research, and the way it is packaged, marketed and disseminated.[1]

But little has changed in terms of the research model offered to students and researchers in textbooks. For example, Suzanne Hood *et al.* (1999:3) describe the stages of the process as: 'design, funding, access, fieldwork, analysis and output', while other authors omit even discussion of writing up (Bowling 2002; Denscombe 2002). Given this background, it is perhaps not surprising that David Silverman (1999: 273) concludes that: 'The idea that social research might influence public policy provides an inspiration for many young social scientists. In most English-speaking countries the sad truth is that things have never worked in this way.'

In this book, we question the limited conception of the end point of the research process found in most texts. We argue that the research model needs to be extended and that this has implications for the whole process. We believe that social researchers should – and often do in practice – pay greater attention to and take greater responsibility for the outcomes of research than is apparent in most accounts of the research process. This goes beyond just producing 'outputs', although it raises more questions than are usually addressed in the textbooks about the complexities of making findings available. It includes engagement with processes of application and implementation of findings in policy and practice. We make the case that in social research these elements should be considered as an integral part of the research process, as much part of the research plan as setting aims and deciding methods, rather than detached activities which take place after the 'real' research has been completed. Moreover, this is not just a matter of extending the end stage of the research process, and has implications for funders and commissioners of research as well as other stakeholders. When we talk about extending social research, we mean extending the scope of every stage and the roles of all the actors as a consequence of taking the end product more seriously. Paying proper attention to impact affects every aspect of the research process. The key principles underlying our approach are set out in brief in Table 1.1.

TABLE 1.1 Extending social research – key principles

Social research unavoidably changes the human condition. It follows that these are the key principles of extending social research.

1   Extending social research places a spotlight on the impact of the research process and the research product.
2   Extending social research expands the research process to include reporting, applying, publicizing and implementing research findings.
3   All stages are extended. Extending social research requires rethinking the whole process.
4   Research relationships are extended as funders, partners, expected beneficiaries and end users are engaged as partners in the change process.
5   Researchers' roles are extended as they take responsibility for what happens with their findings.
6   Researchers' skills are extended as they focus on the change process.

In making these arguments, we are not claiming that our ideas or approaches are unique. Other researchers have drawn attention to this gap (for example, Fox 2003; Hughes 2003a). And, as we have already indicated, there is substantial attention being paid to the question of how research can be more effectively used to influence policy making and practice through the process of 'knowledge transfer' (HM Treasury 2004) or through a strengthened and more accessible 'evidence base', sometimes supported by extensive institutional mechanisms such as the National Institute for Clinical Excellence or the Social Care Institute for Excellence in the UK. However, these major developments in research and 'dissemination' practice have had relatively little impact on accounts of the research process by methodologists.

What we are aiming to do is:

- to bring together a disparate literature about enhancing the impact of research in a new way;
- to move the focus of attention in discussing impact from what happens after research is completed to making it a central factor in the whole research process;
- to illustrate and debate the implications of this shift through the critical discussion of practice examples of mainly locally based research drawn from our experience.

We are critically engaging with existing models of the research process but are not arguing for the privileging of one model – for example, action research – over others. Indeed, we would argue that, while our arguments are not compatible with all the assumptions underlying different models of research, they are widely relevant. All social research should grapple with issues of relevance, applicability and impact.

In the remainder of this chapter we introduce some of the main arguments of the book. We explore in a preliminary way the disjunction between the current emphasis on research utilization amongst research funders, policy makers, practitioners and others and the limited consideration of this in research methods texts. We examine the place of the tasks of publication, application and implementation within the research process (what the UK National Health Service's Strategic Development Organization describes as 'communication and development' (Fulop 2001)). We explain that this book is entitled *Extending Social Research* because attention to these tasks involves rethinking every stage of the research process and has a variety of implications for relationships between researchers and other stakeholders. We outline how the book is structured and how it draws on the experience of a multidisciplinary set of social scientific researchers linked with the Centre for Social Justice at Coventry University.

Current models of social research

In recent years, there has been a plethora of research accounts and texts in the social sciences highlighting the contradiction between the classic presentation of social research as 'static, hygienic and orderly' and the actuality of doing social research (for example, Stanley and Wise 1993; Hood *et al.* 1999; Letherby

2003a). Amongst other things, more contemporary accounts focus on issues of emotional involvement and emotion work, power and empowerment within the research process as well as relationships between the self and the other, insiders and outsiders (for example, Wilkinson and Kitzinger 1996; Ribbens and Edwards 1998; Hood *et al.* 1999; Lee-Treweek and Linkogle 2000; Letherby 2003a). Thus, the 'quest for science' has been replaced by a concern to demonstrate the significance of the process for the product, what one of us has called the doing/knowing relationship (Letherby 2004). In part, these approaches involve a critique of the scientific approach to social research (often referred to as positivism)[2] and they support the argument that every aspect of the research process is political (Fox 2003). They reflect our understanding that just as the researcher is likely to affect the research setting so the research setting is likely to affect the researcher. These issues are explored in greater detail in Chapter 3.

Despite these explorations of the complexities and meanings of the research process, the issues of what happens beyond the writing or publication of 'findings' has been little developed in research methods textbooks. Roberts's (1984) complaint about the lack of both quality and depth in discussions about the publication of research findings still applies to books on methods and methodology today. We could find only Christina Hughes's *Disseminating Qualitative Research in Educational Settings* (2003a) devoting a whole volume to aspects of this issue. Some research methods texts, such as Martin Denscombe's *Ground Rules for Good Research* (2002) and Anne Bowling's *Research Methods in Health* (2002) make no mention of publication or even of the task of 'writing up'. Others, for example Roger Gomm's *Social Research Methodology* (2004), scarcely consider what happens once the analysis of fieldwork or other data collection has been written up. Gomm gives less than four characteristically forthright pages to the ethics of publication and the impact of research. Perhaps there is a connection between this lack of attention and his conclusions that '[t]he fate of the large majority of published research is to sit on library shelves unread' (317) and that 'It is not at all clear what effect social research has on policies, practices and public thinking' (319).

The final stage of producing 'output' is variously described by other authors as 'writing up' (Edwards and Talbot 1994: v; Silverman 1999: xi; Denscombe 2003: Contents page), 'writing theses and monographs and giving talks' (Strauss and Corbin 1990: Contents page) or 'reporting and presenting the findings' (Ritchie and Lewis 2003: 287). And some authors draw attention to the view that researchers may consider even writing up (never mind any more extended concern with what happens with research findings) as something to be 'tacked on' (Terre Blanche and Durrheim 1999: 173) or 'tagged on . . . once the real research has been completed' (Denscombe 2003: 284).

In these texts that do discuss writing up, there is a recognition that different kinds of writing and presentation are required for different audiences or by different funders and that alternative modes of presentation – written, oral, diagrammatic – should be adopted to aid communication. Even so the variety of methods is surprisingly limited, still rarely, for example, discussing the use of drama, video, websites or other forms of active and interactive communication to present material or the involvement of research respondents in writing or presenting findings. Relatively few writers perceive the act of (re)presentation of research as a necessarily political act, an intervention rather than a description. So there is often little sense of ethical responsibility for how findings might be read, interpreted or applied, or of obligations to research respondents or other stakeholders. Indeed, postmodern accounts of research can serve to distance the researcher further from how texts are read and interpreted (Alvesson 2002). It is, perhaps, not by chance that the frequently used concept of 'dissemination' originated as a word implying the scattering of seed with little sense of responsibility for the consequences! (See Note 1 for further explanation.)

Some believe that social research should not be political. For example, Martyn Hammersley and Roger Gomm (1997: 51) argue that taking a political stance and adopting an 'active commitment to some other goal than the production of knowledge' means that research is guilty of bias and 'culpable systematic error'. For us, as we argue in Chapter 3, no research, no process of knowledge production, can be free from ideological influences: research is unavoidably political. However, even where no claim to objectivity or neutrality is made, the 'normal', limited model of the research process which terminates in writing up often suggests a distance or separation between the researcher, the material that is the subject of their research and the audience that the writing (or presentation) addresses. For example, Denzin and Lincoln argue that qualitative research 'consists of a set of interpretive, material practices that make the world visible' (2003a: 4) and that in the 'terminal phase' of qualitative analysis the researcher 'assesses, analyses, and interprets the empirical materials that have been collected', producing 'interpretations, which are then integrated into a theory or put forward as a set of policy recommendations' (2003b: 419). It is not that Denzin and Lincoln think that the researcher is neutral or absent – they argue for qualitative inquiry to be re-engaged as a form of 'radical democratic practice' (2003b: 422) – but the language suggests a divide between research and practice resulting, perhaps, from the persistent tentacles of the 'scientific' model, the continuing privileging of the idea of objectivity. Similarly, Clarissa White *et al.* (2003: 287) argue that the 'reporting task, therefore, is not simply an act of recording the outcomes of the analysis but also an active construction and representation of the form and nature of the phenomena being explored'. This task of representation is seen as complex, allowing for further consideration of the data and requiring care to ensure that the findings are accessible to the 'audience' (288). However, in each case the researcher is an observer, a commentator on the world into which he or she enters, a reporter from the front line, even though the process of presentation is recognized to be subtle and sophisticated.

In contrast, we – like others – believe that the overt positioning of the researcher in relation to the research process and the presentation and publication of research accounts is a fundamental ethical and political responsibility

(Stanley 1993; Humphries 1997; Letherby 2003a; writings in the journal *Auto/ Biography*). Locating oneself within the politics of research production is not only inevitable – it is required. This reflects the view that: '[t]he social scientist is not some autonomous being standing outside society. No-one is outside society, the question is where he [sic] stands within it . . .' (Mills 1959: 204). In that sense, engagement is inevitable, not a choice. It should be embraced.

Some texts and some models do clearly identify the issue of the impact of social research as an issue for the research process, in particular those that attempt to develop 'action' and/or 'emancipatory' research approaches. For example:

> Interactive social science research may be regarded as a pragmatic, utilitarian or user-orientated approach to research (Bee Tin, 1989) and incorporates a value-base that is committed to promoting change through research. It is democratic and participatory by nature and is in sharp contrast to the positivistic 'top-down' approach which has been accused of 'lifting decisions from the village square' and placing them with 'experts or outside agencies' (Bryant, 2001). The practice goes by many names: community-based research, participatory research, collaborative research, and others, but rests on two main principles: democratization of the knowledge process, and social change (Stoeker, 1996). Action research forms part of this genre, and is associated with attempts to bring about emancipation and social justice based on the desires and direct involvement of ordinary people (Fisher, 1994).
>
> (Todhunter 2004: unpaginated)

> You do find women with a foot in both camps who recognize the need for campaigners to utilize academic research and for academics to actively put energy into translating what they know into action. My experiences of the Zero Tolerance campaign and other campaigns show that when this happens sparks can fly!
>
> (Hart 1997: 96)

And even those not adopting these models sometimes explicitly address the issue of impact. For example, Darlington and Scott (2002: 177) include an Epilogue entitled 'From research to practice, programs and politics' in which they argue that researchers can and should be influential in 'determining the impact of their study'. However, here, too, there is a clear distinction drawn between the researchers' role and that of 'managers, policy makers and practitioners' (Darlington and Scott 2002: 177) and the focus of the Epilogue is on the task of making recommendations, a language which itself can reinforce the sense of distance between researcher and application. Interestingly, Darlington and Scott (2002: 188) conclude by asserting that 'research is rarely a linear process and it often takes the researcher down unexpected pathways. The impact of the research may start very early on, and be part and parcel of the research itself, even in studies which are not thought of as "action research".'

As noted earlier, we are not suggesting that our arguments for engagement with the political aspects of research and the research process are unique. What we are advocating, though, is that all academics (not only those engaged in explicitly identified action or emancipatory research) have a responsibility to engage with the political aspects of the research process and products and the change potential of the work they do. Not engaging consciously with the process and the outcomes of research cannot remove responsibility from researchers for the consequences of their work (although, of course, we are not suggesting sole responsibility). This includes responsibility for the consequences when findings that could have had an impact are not made known, or are made known to some constituencies of interest but not others. A conscious engagement with research outcomes – the research products – requires – in our view – that we extend our conception of the research process.

Ending or extending social research?

In textbook research models, then, the end point of research, the product, has usually been seen as the research report and, perhaps, the oral presentations and publications through which findings are made available. The research that many textbooks appear to have in mind is the doctoral thesis, rather than the everyday work of social researchers which is usually shorter term, contractual and often local and in which theory, while vitally important, is less visibly prominent. By contrast, we are arguing for models of the research process to include active engagement with the impact of research.

We are not just arguing for more attention to be paid to 'dissemination', nor just for another stage on the end of a linear conception of the research process. Hughes (2003b: 40) argues that considerations of:

> dissemination [are] present at the very moment of conceptualizing research and continue . . . well after the formal stages of the research are complete . . . This view of dissemination, my view if you like, suggests that dissemination is not simply an end or beginning point but is central to the processes of knowledge production.

This is also our view. That is why we describe our work as 'extending' the applied social research process rather than focusing solely on the 'ending'.

For us this goes far beyond reporting findings as clearly as possible or making recommendations for policy makers or practitioners to consider at arm's length. Rather it requires researchers to engage with funders, policy makers, service providers, practitioners and respondents or service users[3] in considering how research findings can bring about change in policy and practice and in people's lives. We describe this process as one of engagement because what is involved is not just a straightforward or one-way process of application or implementation. The relationship between research findings and practice is rarely that simple. Nor are we suggesting that researchers can act alone but in partnership with other research stakeholders.

We are proposing that this way of thinking about research has an influence throughout the process from the development of research ideas to how research is set up, the relationships with funders, collaborators and respondents during the research programme and the ways researchers engage with processes of reporting and presenting findings, making recommendations, application and implementation. Extending social research is not just about extending the end stage of research, about lengthening the research process, but influences every stage, includes additional work for and with research funders, partners and respondents, and necessitates not only a revision of the traditional research 'model' but a challenge to many accepted and expected academic working practices.

There are three main elements in this argument. First, the business of translating research findings into policy and practice is widely recognized to be a complex and circular process rather than a simple, linear one. The relationship between research and practice is not just a matter of 'knowledge' being put out by researchers and then taken up and applied by policy makers and practitioners (Walter *et al.* 2004a; Noffke and Somekh 2005). Leaving aside until Chapter 3 the conceptual issue of the relationship of research to 'knowledge' (Fox 2003), some work does not easily lend itself to application; findings can be ambiguous or conflictual; policy makers and practitioners may not be aware of the work; it may be known but not understood or misinterpreted, and there are many other barriers to implementation. Given this complexity and evidence about what increases the impact of research, we, like Hughes (2003b), suggest that researchers who are concerned about the outcomes of research need to start considering their utilization strategy early in the process. For example, if the costs of publication and presentation have not been built into the research budget – or into the commissioner's budget – they are unlikely to happen. If time has not been set aside (and costed) for work with service providers or policy makers on application and implementation then researchers will usually have to move on to the next project.

Second, enhancing the utility of research is not just something that has to be thought about at an early stage; it affects every stage of the process. As we will argue below, maximizing awareness and impact requires researchers to build additional activities into the research. For example, Hughes (2003b) rightly questions the boundaries of what she calls 'dissemination', pointing out that processes such as qualitative interviewing cannot take place without some exchange of ideas between researcher and respondent. Just raising questions starts a process of reflection and boundaries cannot easily be drawn between this and more formal processes of reporting findings to respondents or others. Moreover, we are suggesting, researchers have responsibilities for the application and implementation of their work that do not end when the report is written. One of the reasons why some research is felt to be of little use by the non-academic world is the lack of dialogue during the process and, especially, after the research has been reported. Our understanding of when the research process ends needs to be extended.

Third, extending the research process as we are suggesting enhances the quality of the research itself. Hazel Qureshi (2004: 20) argues that:

> In the zone of complexity where uncertainty is high and agreement about action is low, complexity science suggests that useful tools are multiple approaches and iterative trial and error . . . Evidence is helpful, but rarely determines precisely what should be done to reach goals. Useful tools include the feedback loop – to check out results and change future actions accordingly – and a conception of 'good enough' planning.

Not only is the application of findings improved by a process of testing, but the validity of the 'results' themselves will also be enhanced if researchers can see what happens when their evidence is turned into action. This always produces new data that can be fed into the analysis and may modify earlier conclusions. If conclusions are confirmed rather than challenged, they emerge with greater weight and if challenged this indicates the need for further exploration and examination.

What we are proposing is a model, not a prescription. The full range of activities and considerations we discuss will not always be possible or even appropriate. Some commissioners may not want findings to be made widely available, for example when a piece of research is contributing to internal organizational development. Sometimes, knowledge rather than change is the primary concern. But we believe that the issues we raise should always be part of researchers' agendas, part of their thinking as they approach the earliest discussions of the research task or the first stages in the development of a proposal.

Authorship and structure

The ideas that we write about in this book arise, in large part, from research undertaken under the umbrella of the Centre for Social Justice at Coventry University.[4] The members of the Centre who have contributed to the writing of this book are drawn from a variety of disciplines: criminology, political science, sociology, social policy and social work. The final version of our argument is the product not only of many individual research projects, but of a series of discussions and investigations by the participants in order to clarify our ideas and progress the work. We explored our own and each other's experience of research processes as well as examining literature that we found relevant. The primary authors are Gayle Letherby, who was Deputy Director of the Centre from 2001 to 2005 and Paul Bywaters, who was the Director of the Centre from 1998 to 2006. We have drawn on the work of our colleagues, but it is the two of us who have constructed the final text. We have identified particular authors with Chapters 5–8 (in Section 3 of the book) to indicate their major contributions, but all have been involved in developmental discussions which go beyond the confines of a single chapter.

The Centre's orientation towards producing change, on action as well as understanding, resulted in our becoming increasingly involved in the application and implementation of findings in our projects, although this was already our understanding of what research was primarily for. For example, one of us, Gayle Letherby, led a series of projects focusing on teenage pregnancy and young parenthood (see Chapter 5 and subsequently for more details). She and her colleagues on these projects have become active members of local Teenage Pregnancy Partnership Boards. Through that forum and through developing training materials and training sessions with young parents, they have been directly involved in translating research findings into practice. Others of us have been involved in, for example, the development of drama, DVDs, training packs and guidance documents in working with funding partners to turn findings into action (see Chapters 7 and 8). But our ideas are also a product of less satisfactory experiences, when relationships with commissioners did not produce good outcomes and both research funds and effort seemed wasted (Chapter 6). Throughout this period we have had a growing understanding of the importance of involving service users in research processes. Service users have been particularly clear that they want to see concrete action as the end of the research process.

Because it is our most frequent experience, the examples we use throughout the book, and particularly in Section 3 of the book, *Process and product: practice examples* (Chapters 5–8), are mainly of local rather than national or international projects. This is not because the same issues about publication, application and implementation are not relevant; on the contrary. But for many researchers it is this scale of activity that will be most resonant. Because of the development process we have used and who we are, the examples we draw on are mostly UK-based. But we see our work as having relevance across international boundaries.

Following this introductory chapter, in the second section of the book, *Theoretical and practical issues*, we outline and discuss in more detail the epistemological, political and practical significance of extending social research. We both state our position and provide a philosophical background to the approach we are proposing. In Chapter 2, *Extending social research: why?*, we broaden and deepen the arguments outlined here for adopting this extended research model. We explore the ethical, pragmatic and methodological arguments as well as key barriers, problems and challenges. For example, while the current UK government's belief in evidence-based policy making is part of the pragmatic case for researchers focusing more attention on outputs and outcomes, other dimensions of government policy act as barriers. The quality assurance and funding mechanisms currently in place for university-based research, in particular the Research Assessment Exercise, favour impact within the academic community over making a difference in the policy and practice world, despite some attempts to increase the recognition of applied research. Academic promotion similarly depends more on publication to audiences of academic peers than on application or presentations that make work more widely available.

In Chapter 3, *Extending social research: meanings and understandings*, we look behind the reasons for adopting an extended research model to the underpinning epistemological and methodological assumptions on which it is based. The relevance of concepts such as standpoint and praxis, objectivity and subjectivity, reliability, validity and generalizability, insider and outsider are examined.

Our ideas about what extending social research would mean in practice are explored in more detail in Chapter 4, *Extending social research: how?* We develop the argument that the whole research process is affected and indicate what this means for funders, other stakeholders and researchers. The importance of building this approach in from the start of the commissioning or design process, the implications for methods and reflexivity in the process are all part of this discussion.

In Section 3, *Process and product: practice examples*, we explore what the extended model of the research process means in practice by drawing on a range of examples. In this section, which has been written by the group of researchers linked to the Centre for Social Justice, the chapters are divided in terms of four aspects of the research process: *Setting the agenda, Managing the process, Outputs* and *Outcomes*. Within this structure we discuss issues of power and involvement, roles, skills and methods in the research process as they relate to the relationships between funders, researchers and respondents. We look at how an extended model influences the work between these stakeholders, examining how research ideas emerge and receive financial support, the contracting process, the place of advisory or steering committees and the implications for participation by research respondents and communities of interest. We consider alternative methods and media through which research findings can be made known, the skills and tasks involved and the obstacles faced. Finally in this section, we look at how researchers can contribute to application and implementation, to translating findings into action and, again, explore barriers.

In the final section of the book, *Reflections*, we consider further the issues raised by the arguments and evidence we have presented and the policy context in which social science research takes place. We return to the implications for researchers and other stakeholders and finish by reviewing what we have learned from writing the book. There is a particular focus on the enhanced range of skills that are required by the extending research approach.

End points

Social research has rarely been taken more seriously, in the UK at least. As we have argued, government at local and national levels, policy makers and professional practitioners in health, education, social services and other spheres formally acknowledge and support the case for evidence-based policy and practice (for example, Blunkett 2000), even if there remains debate about the kinds of evidence and problems of application (Webb 2001). This is perhaps the moment to share in Anthony Giddens's optimism, although we (and others – see Chapter 2) do not think it is sociology alone that can make this claim:

> The practical impact of social sciences is both profound and inescapable. Modern societies together with the organizations that compose and straddle them are like learning machines, imbibing information in order to regularize their mastery of themselves . . . Only societies reflexively capable of modifying their institutions in the face of accelerating social change will be able to confront the future with any confidence. Sociology is the prime medium of such reflexivity.
>
> (Giddens 1999: 21)

By reflecting on our practice, we hope to open up debates about the purpose and process of social research and the role of researchers. Perhaps, if we shift our way of conceptualizing the research process, both aspiring and experienced researchers can realistically expect that what they do will make a difference, not just to themselves and their research colleagues, but to the wider societies of which we are members.

Notes

1. The word 'dissemination' is used widely by researchers to describe the presentation of research material just as the word 'seminal' is used to describe a ground-breaking piece of research or writing. Both 'dissemination' and 'seminal' have their roots in the word 'semen' ('the impregnating fluid of male animals') with the definition of dissemination being 'to scatter abroad as in sowing seed'. We prefer to avoid using these words because in origin they are both misleading and gendered.

2. Ann Oakley (1999: 65) suggests that there is confusion over the term positivism and that 'Anyone who believes that hypotheses need to be warranted, anyone who uses numerical data or statistics, anyone who is concerned about representativeness or generalizability or the credibility of research findings is liable to be deemed a "positivist".' It is important to remember that positivism and the use of quantitative methods are not necessarily the same thing.

3. We recognize that the term 'service users' is inadequate to describe constituencies, communities of interest or members of social movements who wish for an involvement in decisions and processes that affect their lives whether decisions by service providers, researchers or others. The user movement encompasses those excluded from receiving services and those who choose not to use services as well as those who are past, present or future potential service users. We realize that we are also referring to those whose identity is not bound up in service use but in political or social categories whether chosen or imposed. We employ the term here partly to distinguish it from 'end users' or 'research users', terms which have been used primarily to refer to public or private sector organizations and individuals who make use of research findings in developing their products, policies or practices. We do not separate out carers from service users, but rather see carers as also being actual or potential users or refusers of services. We apologize for using this convenient but inadequate shorthand.

4. The Centre for Social Justice at Coventry University was founded in 1998 and was active until 2006 when it became part of a larger research grouping in the University, SURGE – the Applied Research Centre in Sustainable Regeneration.

Section 2

THEORETICAL AND PRACTICAL ISSUES

2

Extending social research: why?

Gayle Letherby and Paul Bywaters

Introduction • Reasons for extending social research • Barriers, problems and challenges to extending social research • End points

Introduction

This chapter is the first of three within which we provide an outline of the epistemological, political and practical significance of extending social research. Thus, here we begin to consider the theory and practice of our suggested model.

Nick J. Fox (2003) identifies three main reasons why research is not translated into practice: first there is the conservative view that practitioners know best and should be left to get on with it; second is the evidence-based practice approach which suggests that practitioners are lacking in key knowledge and require re-education; third is the view that the fault lies with the model of research developed in academia and the researcher should change working practices. Focusing on the latter, Fox argues that because evidence is contingent and needs to be contextualized, the way forward is *practice-based research*, a model influenced by post-structuralism and action research. Louise Locock and Annette Boaz (2004: 381) suggest that the practice-based approach requires caution on a number of grounds. First, it is based on the questionable assumption that practitioners would want to be involved in research. Second, it risks undervaluing the importance of practice-based knowledge as being distinct from research. Finally, it risks devaluing the skills of professional researchers. Locock and Boaz (2004) conclude by stating that the research community has the potential to support other practitioners, but that difference and distance are often strengths. The distinct skills of research, policy and practice communities should be acknowledged and valued, rather than research becoming subordinate to the interests of policy makers. Like Locock and Boaz (2004) we argue for the political professional significance of academic research and in the main body of this chapter we focus on the reasons for extending social research and the challenges and barriers to this. We consider the three main kinds of arguments for extending social research beyond the traditional model: ethical, pragmatic and methodological. As well as being significant individually these are also interrelated. We then consider some intellectual, practical and institutional tensions to extending social research.

Reasons for extending social research

Ethical arguments

As we have already argued in Chapter 1, we believe that research is inalienably and inevitably political. Berry Mayall *et al.* (1999) agree and argue that research involves three intersecting interests: those of researchers, of research respondents and of those individuals, groups and institutions with the power to influence research priorities through funding, policy making and other processes. Mayall *et al.* (1999) characterize the second and third elements of this triumvirate in terms of social disadvantage and dominance but this is not necessarily or exclusively the case.

The central and overarching reason for extending social research is, therefore, that researchers have a moral obligation to take into account the impact of their work on others. While social research often acts in the interests of dominant groups, it operates in a context in which various kinds of power are exercised and negotiated. It is not always the case that 'advantaged groups . . . are not commonly available for critical scrutiny . . . [and that respondents need to be] protected from research by powerful majority interests' (Mayall *et al.* 1999: 1). It is important not to over-pacify respondents and to recognize that the 'researcher as all powerful and respondents as powerless' assumption is simplistic and power is fluid and negotiated within research (e.g. Millen 1997; Collins 1998; Letherby 2003a). Yet, much social research has an impact on the lives of people researched and on the lives of people other than respondents and researchers have an ethical responsibility to consider and take into account the human consequences of their work. (The only exceptions would be those research projects which are carried out entirely without the involvement of respondents and which are unreported: conditions which themselves raise ethical questions.)

A cursory survey of recent writings in various disciplines and traditions and from various countries suggests that we are not the only ones concerned with the impact and outcome of research beyond the traditional end point of presentation of findings. For example, Ian Butler (2002: 243) demonstrates this in discussing the development of a code of ethics for social work research. The principle of 'respect of autonomy . . . implies treating others as moral agents in their own right, as ends in themselves and not simply as means' (243). The principles of 'beneficence and non-maleficence' require the researcher to consider consequences for all affected parties and this goes beyond those immediately involved such as respondents or funders. The principle of 'justice' requires consideration of the balance of interests between the researcher and others and between parties affected by any research. Each of these points has a bearing not only on the traditional foci of research ethics: informed consent, confidentiality and so on, but also on the impact of those involved in some way with the researchers as well as the consequences of research findings. Butler's code of ethics includes a number of clauses of relevance to this argument including the following:

2. Both the process of social work/care research, including the choice of methodology, and the use to which any findings might be put, should be congruent with the aims and values of social work practice . . .

6. In establishing the aims and objectives of their research, social work and social care researchers are to consider the ascertainable consequences of their actions for the users of social work/care services, both in particular and in general in order to ensure that the legitimate interests of service users are not unwarrantably compromised or prejudiced by the proposed investigation.

(Butler 2002: 245–6)

Similarly, for many feminists, feminist research is feminist theory in action: the aim being to understand the world and change it. As Judith Cook and Mary Fonow (1980: 80) note: 'Feminist research is, thus, not research about women but research for women to be used in transforming their sexist society . . .' Thus, feminist research and ultimately feminist theory has political aims in that it celebrates and is grounded in the daily experiences of women (and men), and by focusing on experience it is able to challenge mainstream/malestream knowledge. Analysis is grounded in the experience of respondents although feminists accept that ultimately it is researchers who interpret the data and decide what respondents 'really meant' (e.g. Stanley and Wise 1993; Wilkinson and Kitzinger 1996; Letherby 2003a). Thus, feminist research challenges the claims of 'true' grounded theory but adopts a grounded theoretical 'approach'.

Research informed by feminist principles then has the 'desire' and the 'goal' to 'create useful knowledge which can be used by ourselves and others to make a difference' (Kelly *et al.* 1994: 28). However, it is also important to recognize that:

> Feminism is not a unitary category which encapsulates a consistent set of ideas within an identifiable framework. It is not a neat and coherent phenomenon which can be measured in quantitative terms (Griffin 1989). So, as Griffin notes, the concept of feminism is under continual negotiation and there is not one feminism but many. So, for most women, the identification of oneself as feminist is not straightforward and involves social, political and personal decisions and choices.
>
> (Letherby 2003a: 136)

Which means that it is necessary to be aware of what Stanley (1984: 201) calls 'the conundrum of how not to undercut, discredit or write-off women's consciousness as different from our own'.

Recently sociologists in America, Canada and Britain have been concerned with the presentation of academic work beyond the academy: a discussion also relevant to our extending social research agenda. Michael Burawoy in his 2004 Presidential Address to the American Sociological Association argued for 'public sociology' thus:

> The bulk of public sociology is indeed of an organic kind – sociologists working with a labor movement, neighbourhood associations, communities of faith, immigrant rights groups, human rights organizations. Between the organic public sociologist and a public is a dialogue, a process of mutual education. The recognition of public sociology must extend to the organic kind which often remains invisible, private and is often considered to be apart from our professional lives. The project of such public sociologies is to make visible the invisible, to make the private public, to validate these organic connections as part of our sociological life.
>
> (Burawoy 2005: 8–9)

Burawoy and others in America and Britain argue for a special place for sociology and sociologists within the social sciences as 'public intellectuals'. For example, in Britain John Scott (2005) (a sociologist influenced by C. Wright Mills's *Sociological Imagination*) argues:

> The core concerns of the sociological imagination have to be sustained within the sociology curriculum. There is a general framework of ideas about social relations that may be the *common* concern of the social sciences but is the *particular* concern of sociology. Professional sociology is the specific guardian of these intellectual concerns ... This intellectual

task centres on the idea of what it is to talk about human 'society' in all its complexity.

(Scott 2005: 7.2)

(See also other articles in the 'Future Trends' debate in *Sociological Research Online*, 2005, Vol. 10 and 2006, Vol. 11.)

In Canada Caelie Frampton *et al.* (2006), in their edited collection of essays on political activist ethnography, credit their approach to the sociologist Dorothy Smith:

> As an approach to producing a reliable knowledge of the social in order to facilitate transformative aims, political activist ethnography finds its roots in the work of Dorothy E. Smith. Contrary to the premises of official sociology, which aims to explain people using categorical abstractions like 'socialization', 'social roles and norms' or 'dysfunctionality', D. Smith developed what she called institutional ethnography as a sociology for women, for the oppressed and – ultimately – for people (D. Smith 1987, 1999, 2005) . . . institutional ethnography shows how the practices of ethnography can be turned against the ruling institutions in our own society.
>
> (Frampton *et al.* 2006: 6)

Also in Canada, Joanne Martel (2004: 179) – a criminologist – makes a claim for criminology as the discipline most closely linked to policy and politics:

> Nowhere, perhaps, is the production of knowledge more enmeshed with social policies and political agenda than in criminology. Criminological research either feeds criminal justice policies and practices, participating in their exponential growth, or it critiques them. One way or another, though, criminological research is inseparable from what Nils Christie (1994) refers to as the industry of crime control. Thus criminological 'science' is embedded in political realities that tend to steer knowledge construction away from epistemological orientations that could threaten the field's very existence and relevance to punitive contemporary politicise about crime and punishment.

Here we do not intend to make a case for any discipline or approach to claim greater social relevance than others; rather we present these varied methodological and political concerns and pronouncements as evidence of the support for the ethics of extending social research beyond traditional models. The scholars (and others like them) reported above argue for social science research to make a difference. What we do in this book is consider ways in which this can happen.

Pragmatic arguments

In addition to the ethical benefits of extending social research there are also pragmatic arguments prompted not least by recent government concerns and funding drivers. Thus, some obligations are contractual or a matter of self-interest rather than ethical. Put simply, if social researchers are to be successful in securing research funding they *have* to pay attention to the publication and application of their findings:

> Competition from the commercial research and consultancy sector has brought home to academic researchers the importance of conducting and communicating research in ways that 'users' (often actually clients who are footing the bill) find helpful. How to structure a report, write in plain English, make a five minute presentation: these are skills which are now seen to be as important as how to design a questionnaire, conduct an interview or analyse data.
>
> (Solesbury 2001: 4)

William Solesbury (2001) has suggested that there are a number of major forces driving the current emphasis on evidence-based practice. Of these, funders are the dominant influence. In the context of social science research, he suggests that funders come into three main categories: government departments as direct funders, the research councils and charities. To this list – not least from our own experience – we would add local government in its various forms and local manifestations of national organizations, such as primary care trusts. Miriam David (2002: 213) notes that the use of social science knowledge for both understanding and transforming social policies and political systems has come to be assumed. In Britain, for example, 'what works' has come to dominate public policy discourses.

The Labour governments of 1997 and 2001 have been particularly pressing in their call for evidence to support policy development, the delivery of policy objectives and the evaluation of policy outcomes. 'Good government is thinking government . . . rational thought is impossible without good evidence . . . social science research is central to the development and evaluation of policy' (Blunkett 2000: 4). This reflects continued concern of a distance between researchers and policy makers:

> It is disappointing that some of the most gifted and creative researchers seem to have turned away from policy-related issues, preferring to work on questions of little interest to those outside of the research community. There is a danger of too much concentration on the micro level – what is the point of research which becomes narrower and narrower, with small groups of people responding to each other's writing in esoteric journals, read only by themselves and relevant only to themselves? This is a dangerous turning which we must try and address. (Section 21.)

To have a practical influence, conclusions from research must be real-istic and achievable. What policy makers find most frustrating and least useful are, at one extreme, a refusal to venture out from behind the safety of the data and the methodology to draw out any policy implications at all; and, at the other extreme, recommendations which may represent the ideal but take no account whatever of issues of costs, achievability, the interaction with other priorities and possible unintended consequences; or conclusions which are just not sufficiently backed up by the evidence. This is ivory-towerism at its worst. (Section 49.)

> (From a speech by David Blunkett to the Economic and
> Social Research Council (ESRC) 2000, cited by
> Locock and Boaz 2004: 376)

Similarly, Blunkett's successor as Secretary of State, Charles Clarke, in a speech in 2003 was critical of the 'medieval concept of the university as a community of scholars unfettered by the difficulties and problems of the wider society' (cited by Locock and Boaz 2004: 376).

Not surprisingly, then, the White Paper, *Modernising Government* (Cabinet Office 1999: Ch. 2, para. 6) called for better use of evidence and research in policy making and led to the establishment of the National Institute for Clinical Excellence and the Social Care Institute of Excellence. Such attitudes have been increasingly apparent in the UK amongst other major research funders, both those closer to direct governmental influence (e.g. the ESRC) and more distant from it (e.g. the Joseph Rowntree Foundation (JRF), the Nuffield Foundation), and are apparent in the RAE 2008's proposal that greater recognition – and different rules – should be given to applied research (HEFCE 2004) (see below).

The thirst for applicable research knowledge on which to base policy has influenced new research and produced the drive to exploit more fully existing data or findings: the systematic review industry exemplified by the Cochrane and Campbell 'Collaborations',[1] funded by a combination of government and large trust funds (www.cochrane.org and www.campbellcollaboration.org). However, these kinds of approaches and those of organizations for promoting evidence-based practice, such as the Centre for Evidence-informed Education Policy and Practice (www.eppi.ioe.ac.uk), Making Research Count (www.uea. ac.uk/SWK/MRC_web/public_html) and Research in Practice (www.rip.org.uk), all depend on a post-hoc application of research findings. It is an industry created to bridge the gap between researchers on the one hand and policy makers and practitioners on the other. However, if researchers gave more attention to issues of application and implementation from the start, less of this post-hoc activity would be necessary. It would also negate the need for an over-bureaucratized research 'industry':

> Evidence-based movements are founded on the principle of raising aware-ness of research findings that could improve services or decision making,

and ensuring that these findings are acted upon. In short, the aim is to improve research impact. This in turn has generated another layer of research and debate concerned with how best to improve research impact.

(Locock and Boaz 2004: 378)

In addition, it is important to remember that 'policy makers might like to believe practitioners want the same as them, but practitioners themselves may want very different things from research, and may view research which they see as serving government interests with suspicion' (Locock and Boaz 2004: 378, see also Packwood 2002). On the other hand, research which does not match government agendas may be dismissed:

The government wants to hear about some evidence and not others. We have lots of research gathered together, indicating that putting students into ability groups does not help results and can hurt students' self-esteem, but the government says grouping is the way forward (Ball in Plomin 2001, cited by Packwood 2002: 270)

We agree with Angela Packwood (2002) and Louise Locock and Annette Boaz (2004) that research that meets government priorities at all times would mean a very restricted research agenda. In addition, as Michael Bloor (1998) suggests, as researchers we need to take care not to become government servants:

Assisting in the extension of outreach work to new populations, or suggesting ways to increase the effectiveness of therapeutic community practice, are each alike analysable as endeavours which tighten the disciplinary grip of experts on citizens. In a new twist on Becker's old 'whose side are we on?' question, it may be argued that sociology should be assisting not in the extension of power, but in the extension of resistance – resistance to meddlesome interference in prostitutes' street dealings, and resistance to expert orchestration of patients' private lives. The opposite of power is not absence, but the resistance it provokes; sociologists, so the argument goes, should be laying the groundwork for citizen resistance than fostering the extension and effectiveness of expert power.

(Bloor 1999: 323)

Thus, we are not suggesting that in order to have our research funded we must compromise our political and academic principles and/or only engage in work that produces practical outcomes to support current political drivers. However, what the mainstream political interest in research and research funding does necessitate is academic debate (such as this) on the parameters and complexities of the research process and products.

Methodological arguments

Our suggested extending social research approach involves three interrelated methodological tenets. The first is the fact that what we do affects what we get; that the process of research affects the research product(s). So, the ways in which we establish study groups and obtain access to respondents; our behaviour when entering and leaving the research field all influence our 'findings' – our 'results'. Furthermore, we need to acknowledge and theorize about the significance of power and emotion during data collection and in analysis and funder/researcher/respondent roles and relationships and identity, including reference to the significance of gender, class, ethnicity, age, accent and other social differences (see Chapter 3 for further discussion).

The second tenet is the one presented earlier: that social research cannot avoid impacting on its funders, respondents and audience and that, therefore, attention should be paid to what influences the kind and extent of impact that research activity and findings have. The 'gold-standard' randomised control trial focuses attention on how the research is set up and data is analysed, but it is then often just assumed that good enough evidence will lead to good enough implementation. Yet, this reflects a simplistic view of both the research process and the translation of findings to outcomes: 'Given the astronomical variety of implementation of even one basic program model, the variety of staff, clients, organizational contexts, social and political environments, and funding levels, any hope for deriving generalizable findings is romantic' (Weiss 2000: 44).

The third tenet is the complexity of the extension of the model: it is not easy to consider how research processes or outcomes have an impact and these issues require attention and study. For example, a striking feature of the literature on improving impact is better ongoing interaction between researchers and users. Michael Huberman (1987) calls for 'sustained interactivity' throughout the research process from the definition of the problem to application of the findings. Similarly, Sandra Nutley (2003: 12) argues that researchers who want their work to be used must pay attention to the gap between research and policy or practice worlds that have: 'different priorities, use different languages, operate to different time scales and are subjected to very different reward systems'.

'Sustained interactivity' between researchers and respondents, collaborators and funders beyond the traditional end point of social research also assists us in understanding the relationship between the process and the product(s) and is relevant to ethical and pragmatic concerns. One way of validating findings from social research is through their application in practice which necessitates the continuation of analysis way beyond the traditional 'recommendations' stage of the research process.

As we noted in Chapter 1, some will see our arguments as applying only to some kinds of research – to 'action research' or 'emancipatory research' – but not to others. There are many definitions of action research (Hart and

Bond 1995), but undoubtedly many features of the way we have described the research process have much in common with action research thinking. However, we are arguing that in any model of ethical social science research, there will be human consequences that researchers are required to consider. Even if research is conducted without substantial stakeholder involvement or human respondents (documentary research, for example) the process of reporting and publication brings with it, we believe, a requirement to reflect on the research process and product(s) and to produce 'accountable knowledge' (Stanley 1991 and see Chapter 3 for further discussion).

Barriers, problems and challenges to extending social research

Lack of skills and opportunity

Extending social research necessitates skills not taught as part of traditional research training, not least in terms of the skills necessary for involvement in effective communication and application of findings. If textbook research models pay little attention to the processes involved in translating findings to outputs and outcomes (see Chapter 1), then research students will not be taught or learn the relevant skills. However, this is not the position of the ESRC training requirements (ESRC 2005a: 3) which require, at least, that post-graduate research students are trained in 'Communication skills: writing, dissemination and media skills' including communicating with non-academic audiences, using the internet and other media and working with 'user' networks. In addition an extended and extending relationship with respondents, funders, commissioners and other stakeholders may also require skills that research training leaves us unprepared for. For example:

> Those who wish to take the path of collaborative research be warned: there is no easy way forward. You and your co-researchers may be attracted to the rhetoric of participation; you may think you are deeply committed to the values of participative relationships. Yet for those of us encultured to unconscious participation the leap to a future reflexive participation is immense: there will be doubt and mistrust, there will be disagreement and conflict, there will be failures as well as success. For the birth of a new more integrated consciousness means the death of the old. Future participation means the loss of the myth of certainty, the loss of control, the tempering of the rational mind. It means learning to trust the wisdom of the unknown other.
>
> (Wilkins 2000: 55–6)

A more serious problem, in some respects, is a lack of funding for translating findings into outputs and outcomes. Some research funders, such as the Joseph Rowntree Foundation (JRF), set aside a ring-fenced element in the research budget for projects they support for the processes of 'dissemination' (see www.jrf.org.uk/funding/research/). However, others rely on researchers to include such costs within budget proposals and, in competitive bidding processes, these costs will often be shaved to secure success. When research is commissioned the actual and associated cost (e.g. in terms of university administration, overheads and the need for full-economic costing)[2] of research undertaken by academics may be prohibitive and researchers may feel that they are working 'above and beyond' even in terms of the traditional model. As Isabel Walter *et al.* (2003) argue, whilst there is some evidence of an increase in research impact arising from strategies aimed at bringing researchers, policy makers and practitioners closer together, differences in culture, goals, information needs, timescales, reward systems and language remain substantial barriers. They suggest that the demands on academics to meet UK Research Assessment Exercise targets (see below) and to satisfy other peer reviewers of their rigour may be at odds with the duty that practitioners have to stay within budget or meet government targets. Their respective reward systems are based on very different requirements. Thus, the costs of working in the way that we suggest are considerable, not just in terms of finance, because they rely significantly on human relationships as well as on the creative use of electronic and other media. The more creative and interactive ways of ensuring that findings make an impact such as drama or video or the development of training materials tend to be more expensive than the production of traditional written reports and articles, but even there paying attention to a variety of audiences takes significant time. (For more on the skills required when extending social research see Chapters 4 and 9).

Academic structures and lack of institutional support

Having briefly identified lack of skill and opportunity in relation to extending social research we turn now to the barriers within the academy. Concern over lack of funding overlaps with concerns about the lack of institutional support. It is widely acknowledged that higher education is perceived as a product and higher education institutions represent a 'service industry'. Universities and the departments within them have business plans; both research and teaching is quality assured (e.g. in the UK there is both a Research Assessment Exercise, and Teaching Quality Assessment) and this external moderation and review has encouraged the development of a particular management focus within institutions to ensure improved performance on the criteria valued by the producers of league tables, which appear in the media (Marchbank and Letherby 2001).

Higher education in the UK in the twenty-first century is affected by both 'New Right' and 'New Left' policy and ideology. The impact of the focus on individualism, consumerism and quality pushed by consecutive Conservative governments from the last 1970s through to the late 1990s has been recognized for some time. For example:

> The Higher Education sector is increasingly being forced into, and, in some cases has willingly adopted the entrepreneurial spirit of the market. One consequence of the move toward entrepreneurialism which most of us are experiencing is a shift towards the stronger 'managerial' culture in Higher Education.
>
> (Epstein 1995: 59–60)

Similarly, with reference to the work of a number of writers from North America, Marilee Reimer (2004: 13) notes:

> Jan Currie and Janice Newson identify globalization as one of the main factors behind the corporate restructuring of universities. They conceptualize globalization as a process that combines 'a market ideology with a corresponding material set of practices drawn from the world of business'. Janice Drakich, Karen Grant and Penni Stewart argue that in the past thirty years academics have seen the introduction of hiring freezes and budget cutbacks – initiatives strongly tied to government objectives. This has meant an onslaught of 'rationalizing' by corporate management and the 'objective proletarianization', or downgrading, of academic work. Lisa McCoy identifies two key trends in the restructuring process: the reorganization of universities to fulfil government and business expectations for the 'knowledge economy', and the emergence of the 'accountability movement', which is imposing systems of accountability on academic work.

In the UK in recent years, despite the increase in student numbers (the Labour government target is that 50 per cent of school leavers access higher education by the year 2010), there has not been a corresponding rise in the numbers of academics. Clearly the more time that staff need to spend with students the less time they will have to spend on their own scholarly development: on research and writing. The impact across the sector is likely to be different because, even though some post-1992 universities 'do well' in terms of securing external monies, the highest 'new' university achievers manage to secure about 10 per cent of the amounts that the highest pre-1992 institutions do. Thus, some institutions have fewer resources to support their staff doing research and the development of a research culture. On the other hand the pressures to 'perform' in research terms are likely to be felt more keenly in pre-1992 universities. In addition to cross-sector differences of experience there are also differences within institutions mitigated by social differences amongst academics. For example, Louise Morley (2005) reflects on the gendered implications of quality assurance and audit. Drawing on a study with women academics and academic managers across the higher education sector who all had, at the time of interview, an involvement in audit, she suggests that quality assessment procedures appear to reinforce gendered divisions of labour and employment regimes in the academy. Morley argues that evidence suggests that teaching quality is female-dominated and research quality is male-dominated, prompting her to suggest that there is a morality of quality with women heavily responsible for student-focused services.

With the above in mind we would suggest that the current structures of academia devalue our alternative approach. For the full-time academic the 'quality audit' research agenda is relevant here. Research activity in universities which, as we see, in the UK as elsewhere are increasingly being run on business models, depends on researchers securing external funding against a background of progressively less unit cost funding (DfEE 1997). Heavy cuts in university expenditure have been accompanied by a desire by government to impose top-down bureaucratic and managerialist types of control over academic work (e.g. see Morley and Walsh 1995; Morley 2003) and 'Proof of performance and productivity requires outputs that can be measured and be made visible' (Strathern 1997 cited by Mace 2000). Although the UK RAE 2008 guidance (see above) declares that applied research will be more highly rated, many researchers will be anxious that time spent on turning research findings into social change will be time spent away from writing proposals for funding and work on traditional research outputs – e.g. journal articles, single authored books, book chapters – which count for a high percentage of the allocated star rating of the research unit of assessment. Of course, these strictures are not confined to the experience of UK academics and the concept of 'impact' factor widely used in international assessments of research quality relates to recognition in academic journals and not at all to impact on the human subjects of study, which once again mitigates against an extended social research model.

Yet, with all these pressures in mind, we need to take care that in arguing for the extension of social research we do not make another rod for our own backs. As Bronwyn Davies (2006: forthcoming) argues:

> . . . as I write, the Australian government is establishing yet another twist of the panopticon with which to govern academic work. Rather than count the number of papers we publish, the research dollars we bring in and the higher degree students we graduate, we have to make an account of the impact our work has had on the world and the esteem in which we are held. For a high rating impact rating one must have fundamentally altered policy or practice in a particular field, or produced a major identifiable social, economic, industrial or environmental change, locally or internationally. The researcher is widely renowned in industry or the community for this impact. Examples: changes in legislation, amendments to regulatory arrangements, wide take-up of a product, service, process or way of thinking derived from the research, significant impact of take-up of the

research findings (revenue increases, cost savings, changed 'view of the world', technological change or new products).

... I wanted to protest at this model of academic work. What I write, when it is good, works at the edges of thought, it confronts, it spreads out through its capacity to generate new thinking in others ...

Such work is very different from the kind of work that vaunts itself, that seeks proof of its impact in the form of identifiable social, economic and industrial change – identifiable by number (of citations for example) and able to be captured in a 150 word cliché and self-assessment on 3 and 5 point scales.

We are not arguing for a total ban on the pursuit of knowledge for knowledge's sake. We are cautioned by the Australian experience and are concerned that the use or not of our extending social research model could be used as yet another way to measure success or failure. Rather we are arguing for the significance of an extended social research model and the associated 'critical' training and finance and institutional and government support that comes with that. Within this approach research is valued for its political, social significance, not its financial value, and in and of itself then provides a critique of higher education as entrepreneurialism or what Neil Tudiver (1999: 5 writing with reference to the Canadian academy but his point is generalizable) calls the 'corporate university':

Where universities have traditionally operated from a professional model, the corporate university follows a business model: capitalizing on research as an investment, seeking profit from its ventures, and forming partnerships with corporations through equity financing and licensing.

(Tudiver 1999: 5)

For the academic contract researcher time is even more precious than for his or her colleagues with permanent tenure. Researchers in this position routinely have to prepare new bids before they complete the project on which they are working in order to secure continued employment. With this in mind it is not surprising if extending social research is way down the list of priorities for many.

As this section has highlighted, the increased and increasing business focus of academia plus all forms of quality audit work against the extension of social research that we are proposing, despite the rhetoric of research applicability peddled by government and funding councils. Rather, it appears that academics – like other professionals – are not only expected to be more bureaucratically accountable than ever before but more controllable:[3]

The neoliberal systems of government imposed on universities over the last two or three decades have been aimed at making us less dangerous, more

responsive to government, more caught in the economic order that sees us each as economic units to be used and manipulated by government . . .
(Davies 2006)

The concordat between State and profession is, in a sense, being renegotiated . . . the days of self-regulation may be drawing to a close' (Klein 1990: 130). Moving towards public and explicit regulation and accountability is an example of this shift from 'status' to 'contract'. Trusted occupations that once relied on their taken for granted authority are increasingly compelled to demonstrate their ability to meet performance targets. As the performance of teachers, academics, doctors and the like becomes open to scrutiny we see the relentless logic of Weberian rationality at work. What is surprising is not that academics are being subjected to such scrutiny but that it took so long.
(Mears 2001: 18)

Publish and perish: academic publishers and the media

Having argued that bureaucratic accountability works against the extending social research model we end this section by reflecting briefly on how the 'publish or perish' dilemma (Broughton 1994) within higher education is also part of the problem. In order to secure tenure (both in the UK and elsewhere) many academics start their career on short-term research and/or teaching contracts. To achieve promotion it is necessary to publish our work and as noted above this is important in terms of individual and institutional standing/ranking. Furthermore, one of the ways in which our research can make a difference is for it to influence others, and by publishing it we reach a wider audience. As Dale Spender (1981: 188) notes: 'Research that is not in print does not exist' and to give credibility to our work we need to publish it between the covers of a respectable academic journal or book. Furthermore, what gets published influences those who read it and those who write what comes after, so the written word 'establishes the issues in a discipline – constitutes the parameters and defines the terms of the debate' (Spender 1981: 191).

Thus, as Martel (2004) notes, academic knowledge is policed not least through the ideological propensities of scientific journals, the gatekeeping role played by editors of and reviewers of journals and the selectivity of publishers of books. It is these gatekeepers in the academic community who 'set the standards, produce the social knowledge, monitor what is admitted to the systems of distribution, and decree the innovations in the thought, or knowledge or values' (Smith 1978 cited by Spender 1981: 287). The anonymous refereeing system of academic journals and publishing houses (usually both author(s) and reviewers remain anonymous) appoints reviewers who have interest and expertise in the area under consideration. This system, as Morley (1995: 126) notes, 'privileges the silent reader who exerts power over the one who speaks [writes]'. Although most reviewers undertake their responsibilities ethically, if the writer's work represents a challenge to the reviewer's work it is possible for that reviewer to influence the parameters of the debate by suggesting that the writer's work is not good enough (Spender 1981; Morley 1995).

Academic fashions and favours can of course influence what gets published and what does not and this is relevant to topics, methodological and theoretical approaches and to methods and practices. Reporting on a qualitative criminology project focusing on women's experiences of Canadian imprisonment, Martel (2004) notes that, despite sustained efforts to present the study's findings, the study and thus the experience of those interviewed and similarly affected was ignored and delegitimized by several of the audiences it sought to influence. Martel's experience (highlighted by the following two newspaper reports) demonstrates how working with and through the media can sometimes lead to tension:

> The Elizabeth Fry Society has spent $13,000 of taxpayer money to discover that women in solitary confinement are lonely. The study, released yesterday, was panned by Mitch Gray, Alberta director of the Canadian Taxpayers Federation, as a waste of cash.
> (*Edmonton Sun*, 28 January 2000: 20, cited in Martel 2004: 173)

> The study is anchored by [. . .] anecdotal evidence [and] personal stories from unidentified women in unnamed Prairie prisons [which] makes responding to specific concerns difficult. It's a report involving self-reported information from 12 offenders [. . .] talking about their opinions of segregation, that's basically what the report is.
> (*Star Phoenix*, 2 February 2000: A7, cited in Martel 2004: 174–5)

This tension can of course have serious consequences. In this particular case, failure to recognize and validate the knowledge claims promoted led to the experiences of women in prison being further disenfranchizing. However, in order to promote and retain our role as 'public intellectuals' (see above), and in order to continue to try and influence change within an extended social research model, publication within academic and lay press is essential.

Writing specifically about feminist writing as challenging traditional models (but of course relevant to all research and writing that challenges the traditional and the conventional), Liz Stanley and Sue Wise (1993: 137) admonish that:

> . . . all feminists who are involved in writing and research should be more adventurous, more daring, and less concerned with being respectable and publishable . . .

However, this may not be so easy for those whose careers are less established or even for those who represent a challenge to current fashions and favours.

Finally, it is by no means clear that a greater use of public media will mean that research messages are heard accurately. Media attention is created largely by news values rather than research quality, as Tisdall experienced. 'We received over 100 calls (from the media) shortly after a four line paragraph in the University of Glasgow's newsletter announced we had gained the funds for "A View from the Girls" ' (Tisdall 2005: 99). Despite an admirable, proactive and carefully thought-out media strategy, there was great pressure from the media to 'allow' the young women respondents to tell their stories. This could only be managed to a degree and 'Involving children and young people in research dissemination takes time and personal investment, and even then it can raise ethical quandaries' (Tisdall 2005: 101).

End points

In this chapter we have focused on some of the reasons for and problems resulting from extending social research. Not surprisingly, this discussion draws on and highlights different political positions. The resolution of some of the tensions we have noted here are not easy to find. While there is only limited reference within research texts concerning researcher involvement in what we call the extending research process there is a large and growing literature on what makes for effective processes of publication, application and implementation (Davies *et al.* 2000). However, our arguments do not only depend on proven effectiveness but also on other considerations. We would argue that the quality of research as well as its impact is likely to benefit (from an extended research approach) while the ethical considerations place their own obligations on researchers. Given the number of identified practical and institutional barriers to extending social research that we have identified we may seem to be arguing for the impossibility of the development of this model. Indeed, despite the political rhetoric, the opportunities for extending social research are limited in terms of skills, opportunities and structures. In Chapter 4, we return to these issues and review some of the ways in which such obstacles may be overcome. In Section 3 (Chapters 5–8), we discuss examples of our attempts to put the model into practice, both the successes and the failures, and some of the lessons we have learned. Finally, in Chapter 9 we re-examine, with reference to our personal approach, the political context of research practice and pull together arguments about how the extending research approach can be taken forward.

Notes

1. The Cochrane Collaboration is an international not-for-profit organization, providing up-to-date information about the effects of health care and the Campbell Collaboration is an international non-profit organization that aims to help people make well-informed decisions about the effects of interventions in the social, behavioural and educational arenas.
2. From January 2005 UK universities have been required to cost and manage research projects on a full economic costing basis. See Chapter 9 and the Higher Education Funding Council for England *Transparency Review* (HEFCE 2006).
3. We are not arguing against accountable research and research writing (see Chapter 3 for further discussion), nor do we wish to suggest that academics should not be accountable to their employers, their funders or their students in terms of their research, teaching, administrative and pastoral responsibilities. However, we (like others, Curtis 2005; Ford 2006) are concerned by the increased and increasing focus on measures of accountability that seem – in terms of time and effort – to distract us from the very jobs that we are contracted to do.

3

Extending social research: meanings and understandings

Gayle Letherby and Paul Bywaters

Introduction • Knowledge, values and involvement • Process, product and re/presentation • End points

Introduction

Having made the case for extending social research in Chapter 2 and before going on to consider in greater detail how this might be done in Chapter 4, we focus in this chapter on a number of epistemological questions and try to answer these with specific reference to extending social research:

- What is knowledge and who is knowledge for?
- What is the point of research and who is research for?
- How significant is the relationship between 'us' (as researchers) and 'them' (as respondents and, in this case, as commissioners)?

- How representative is research?

Epistemology, simply defined as theory of knowledge and theories of knowledge production, is concerned with what counts as legitimate knowledge and what can be known. Advocating an extended social research approach challenges traditional (and existing) academic epistemologies both in terms of academic knowledge products and academic knowledge production. So the questions above and the answers to them underpin the why and how of our extending social research model and although, as noted in Chapter 2, we are not arguing against the pursuit of knowledge-for-knowledge's sake we are suggesting that the empirical work that we do should be of value, not just in terms of professional academic labour production (Burawoy 2005) but for those it affects. We are also suggesting that an extending social research agenda has implications for what counts as knowledge. As such we support Karl Mannheim's (1968: 258) view that:

> With the peace of mind that comes from the *a priori* premise that epistemology is independent of the 'empirical' social sciences, the mind is once and for all closed to the insight which a broadened empiricism might bring.

And we further argue that attention to the process of empirical research is important not just in terms of its relationship to the knowledge product(s) but also because the process itself is of intellectual and political significance. We start by reflecting on the relationship between knowledge, values and involvement and then go on to consider issues of process, product and re/presentation.

Knowledge, values and involvement

Objectivity, subjectivity and knowledge production

As noted in Chapter 1, Martyn Hammersley and Roger Gomm (1997) argue that taking a political approach to research results in biased and faulty knowledge. Thus, they argue that research should be motivated by the wish to produce the 'truth' and that 'knowledge production' must be systematically forefronted in the collection, analysis and presentation of evidence. We are not the first to question this apolitical approach to social research (e.g. see Temple 1997; Humphries 1998). We are also not the first to suggest that a value-free social scientific method is both impossible and undesirable. As also indicated in Chapter 1, the pronouncements of Charles Wright Mills are relevant to our extending social research approach in that he believed that the social scientist is part of and not apart from society and that the use of personal life experience in intellectual work is an asset rather than a burden:

. . . learn to use your life experience in your intellectual work; continually to examine it and interpret it. In this sense craftsmanship (sic) is the centre of yourself and you are personally involved in every intellectual product which you work.

(Mills 1959: 216)

There are links too with the work of Mannheim, who argued that all knowledge is 'socially rooted':

[t]he proper theme of [the sociology of knowledge] is to observe how and in what form intellectual life at a given historical moment is related to the existing social and political forces.

(Mannheim 1968: 60 footnote)

With further reference to the research process, it has now become common-place for the researcher to locate him/herself within the research process and produce 'first person' accounts. This involves a recognition that, as researchers, we need to realize that our research activities tell us things about ourselves as well as about those we are researching (Steier 1991). Further, there is recognition among social scientists that we need to consider how the researcher as author is positioned in relation to the research process: how the process affects the product in relation to the choice and design of the research fieldwork and analysis, editorship and presentation (Iles 1992; Sparkes 1998; Letherby 2003a).

As Malcolm Williams (2005: 108) argues, if value freedom is impossible then objectivity is itself a value. He argues for the existence of a value continuum and continues:

To be objective in science commits us to values of law. Objectivity, then, is not an homogeneous value and its context will determine its relationship to other values (and therefore what it is in context). This is a key point, because when we talk about objectivity in science we are talking about something different to objectivity in other spheres. But, if my argument about the value continuum is right, then the meaning of objectivity in any discipline will relate to its internal use *and* its use in the relationship of that discipline to the rest of the social world.

(Original emphasis)

Thus, for Williams, objectivity is situated, that is related to value. One of us has made a similar argument elsewhere, arguing for the necessity of 'theorized subjectivity' – a 'value explicit' position which recognizes that 'bias' is inevitable in the research process and that 'it is better to understand the complexities within research rather than to pretend that they can be controlled, and biased sources can themselves result in useful data' (Letherby 2003a: 71). In a critique of this position, Sue Wise and Liz Stanley (2003) suggest that 'theorized subjectivity' retains an objectivity/subjectivity binary and instead advocate what they call fractured feminist foundationalism (Stanley and Wise 1993, 2006; Wise and Stanley 2003), a position that does not dispute the existence of truth and a material reality but acknowledges that judgements about them are always relative to the context in which such knowledge is produced. In response to this Gayle Letherby wrote:

> I do not believe [theorized subjectivity] is predicated upon an objectivity/ subjectivity binary position. Rather it relies on a recognition that, while there is a 'reality' 'out there', the political complexities of subjectivities, and their inevitable involvement in the research/theorizing processes, make a definitive/final statement at best wishful thinking, in practice impossible, but what is possible, desirable and necessary is the theorization of the subjective.
>
> (Letherby 2003b)

Extending social research is an explicitly political approach and as such acknowledges the significance of the importance of theorized subjectivity in terms of what we study, our interpretation of commissioners' concerns, our initial views on the issue under examination, our framing of the questions, our relationship with respondents, our interpretation of the data and our theoretical considerations. These are all affected by who we are and, thus, who we are affects what we 'know'.

Reflecting on the status of knowledge and issues of involvement Barbara Katz-Rothman (1996: 51) goes so far as to suggest that there has been a fundamental shift in methodological thinking where an 'ethic of involvement has replaced an ethic of objectivity'. From this perspective, writing from personal experience rather than from a position of 'detached objectivity' is likely to give the writer 'credentials'. She adds:

> In the circles I travel in now, if you see an article by a colleague on breast cancer you write to see how she is, wonder when she was diagnosed. If you see an article on Alzheimer's you assume someone's got a parent or in-law to help. I can track my colleagues' progression through the life cycle, through crises and passages, by article and book titles.
>
> (Katz-Rothman 1996: 51)

This, we would suggest, is going rather too far. The ability to draw and reflect on one's own physical experiences and intellectual resources can allow connections to be made and rapport to be developed during fieldwork. Yet, it is not always possible or desirable to research issues close to us. Furthermore, identification should not be seen as a prerequisite to 'good' research. Thus, we think it inappropriate to assume that *all* research is grounded in the autobiography of researchers. In addition, researchers do not always identify with respondents and visa versa even when they share an experience and/or identity (Letherby and Zdrodowski 1995). So we are not suggesting that researchers have to draw on their own life experiences to do good work but that their life experiences are present at some level in all that they do and that it is important to acknowledge this. Thus:

> Self and Other are knottily entangled . . . researchers are always implicated at the hyphen . . . By working the hyphen [between Self and Other], I mean to suggest that researchers probe how we are in relation with the contexts we study and with our informants, understanding that we are multiple in all those relations.
>
> (Fine 1994: 72)

And:

> . . . respondents have their own view of what the researcher might like to hear. Moreover, we draw on our own experiences to help us to understand those of our respondents. Thus, their lives are filtered through us and the filtered stories of our lives are present (whether we admit it or not) in our written accounts.
>
> (Cotterill and Letherby 1993: 74)

In adopting an approach that advocates continued engagement with issues of relevance, applicability and impact we are challenging, as others have before us, the view that good research is value-free and objective (as traditionally defined). Rather, we would argue that all research is a political endeavour and that in extending social research we engage with, make explicit and attempt to put to good use the inevitable political aspects of the research process and product(s).

'Trust me, I'm a university researcher': power, privilege and accountability

As argued above, acknowledging that research is inevitably political involves an acknowledgement of the personhood of the researcher and a need for the researcher and writer to locate her/himself in written accounts. From this perspective all research accounts can be seen as representations of reality and should be open to critical analytical enquiry. With particular reference to feminist praxis, Liz Stanley (1991: 209) describes the relationship between 'intellectual autobiography' and 'accountable knowledge' and the relationship between feminist research and feminist theory thus:

> Feminist theory would be directly derived from 'experience' whether this is experience of a survey or interview or an ethnographic research project, or whether it is experience of reading and analysing historical or contemporary documents. Thus its analysis would centre on an explication of the 'intellectual autobiography' of the feminist researcher/theoretician: it would produce accountable knowledge, in which the reader would have

access to details of the contextually-located reasoning processes which give rise to 'the findings', the outcomes.

Similarly, Ann Oakley (2004: 191) argues:

> ... social scientists have a responsibility to ensure that when they speak about other people, they do so on the basis of warrantable knowledge. The audit trail through research question, methods, data collection, analysis and interpretation needs to be clear, systematic and explicit.

Stanley (1991) and Oakley (2004), then, are insisting that we support our arguments with appropriate evidence, acknowledge other relevant evidence and make transparent the research process; what Zigmunt Bauman (1990) calls 'responsible speech'. But, from our perspective 'accountable knowledge' or 'responsible speech' is not just about making the research process explicit, visible but also about accountability and responsibility in terms of our actions throughout the extended research process. Thus, as we have noted already in earlier chapters, we are accountable to and have responsibilities to all of those who have a stake in and/or are likely to be affected by our research.

Whilst we agree with others who argue that researchers are not intellectually superior to their respondents (e.g. Stanley and Wise 1993) and that everyone theorizes about their lives (e.g. Giddens 1985; Stanley and Wise 1993), we acknowledge the intellectual privilege working in the academy gives us (e.g. Letherby 2002; Abbott *et al.* 2005). Thus, we have access to temporal, material, intellectual and status resources that our respondents and our funders/commissioners often do not have. Indeed, this is sometimes the very reason that research is commissioned. All this of course returns us to the issue of responsibility and accountability in that we need to take care not to abuse the 'epistemic privilege' (the right to be defined as a knower) that our position in the academy gives us. Thus, we must not ignore, dismiss or write out the perspectives, experiences or views of others with whom we come into contact that are different to our own.

We are concerned here, then, with the relationship between knowledge and power. All researchers need to acknowledge the significance of their personhood to the knowledge produced, all researchers need to be clear about how what they have done has affected what they produce and all researchers need to reflect on and take responsibility for the consequences of their research. Thus, we agree with others that to ignore the personal involvement of the researcher within research is to downgrade the personal and we agree that not only is the 'personal political' but the personal is also theoretical and that this is true in terms of what we research, how we research it and in terms of the outputs and outcomes of research.[1]

Process, product and re/presentation

Standpoint and standpoints

Advocating an extending social research approach could be seen as taking a standpoint position in that standpoint epistemologies start with a political focus on experience. Standpoint epistemologists argue that groups of individuals share distinct experiences, that the 'truth' of that experience can be uncovered and that experience is the starting point for any knowledge production and subsequent action (for further explanation see Harding 1993; Millen 1997). It is an approach that foregrounds the standpoint of groups of people when undertaking research and provides a way of looking beyond individual perspectives to challenge stereotypical definitions and perceptions.

Standpoint epistemologies are rooted in foundationalist perspectives based on an insistence that 'truth exists independently of the knower'. Feminist Standpoint Epistemology (FSE), for example, begins from the view that 'masculine' social science is bad social science because it excludes women's experience and suggests the importance of developing a 'successor science' to existing dominant social science paradigms. Thus, FSE starts from the position that the 'personal is political' (see above and Note 1). Some suggest that this perspective draws on Marxist ideas about the role of the proletariat and suggests that women are an oppressed class and as such have the ability not only to understand their own experiences of oppression but to see their oppressors (e.g. see Harding 1987). As Dianne Millen (1997: 7.2) argues, the suggestion is that research based on women's experience provides a more valid basis for knowledge because 'it gives access to a wider conception of truth via the insight into the oppressor'. So, it is not just that the oppressed see more – their own experience and that of the privileged – but also that their knowledge emerges through the struggle against oppression: in this instance the struggle against men.

Standpoint epistemology, though, is not solely the preserve of those concerned with women's experience. Some researchers working in the areas of disability, ethnicity and 'race' and childhood, amongst others, argue for a standpoint approach. When searching for an epistemology based on the experience of African American women, the values and ideas that African writers identify as being characteristically 'black' are often very similar to those claimed by white feminist scholars as being characteristically female. This suggests that the material conditions of oppression can vary dramatically and yet generate some uniformity in the epistemologies of subordinate groups (Hill Collins 1989). Similarly, researchers working in the area of childhood have argued that as both women and children are subject to patriarchy, those in power regard both groups as social problems and both groups find it hard to have their points of view heard and respected (Mayall 2002).

In ways that seem at the same time to both support and challenge our position, supporters of standpoint epistemology suggest that objectivity is possible but that the critical scrutiny of all aspects of the research process is necessary to achieve (what Harding (1993) calls) 'strong objectivity'. This presents a challenge to traditional notions of objectivity which Harding argues are weak because the researchers' own values, assumptions and so on are hidden. So this is not a value-free objectivity but one that recognizes the personhood of the researcher. From this it would seem that Harding's approach is close to ours but there are problems with standpoint epistemology.

One problem with a standpoint approach is that it can imply that one group's perspective is more real, more accurate and better than that of others and if we accept a position which implies that there is only one (real, accurate, best) experience, this can only be built upon the suppression of voices of persons with experiences unlike those who have the power to define that one (real, accurate, best) experience. Further, the view that the more oppressed or more disadvantaged groups have the greatest potential for knowledge implies that the greater the oppression the broader or more inclusive one's potential knowledge. This, in turn, can lead to unproductive discussions about hierarchies of oppression: that is, those who are more oppressed (and how do we prove this anyway?) are potentially more knowledgeable. Even if we find the most oppressed group of all, how do we know that their way of seeing is the 'most true': surely no one particular social location has the complete access to truth? With all of this in mind, once we acknowledge the existence of several standpoints it becomes impossible to talk about 'independent truth' and 'objectivity' as a means of establishing superior or 'better knowledge' because there will always be alternative knowledge claims arising from contextually grounded knowledge of different standpoints. Further, a standpoint position focuses on similarities between people and not differences and so brings with it the danger of viewing a group of people as all the same. Neither women, nor children, nor black people (and so on) are an homogeneous group. We all occupy multiple, combined and intersecting positions of gender, class, ethnicity, dis/ability, sexuality and so on (for further discussion see for example Millen 1997; Letherby 2003a; Abbott et al. 2005).

In advocating an extending social research approach we are not starting from an epistemological position that privileges the knowledge of researchers or (as noted above) from a position that claims to discover or uncover the truth. But neither do we subscribe to a postmodernist epistemology which, in focusing on issues of difference (between people and between understandings and meanings), rejects any claim to knowledge that makes an explicit appeal to the creation of a theory or a truth but rather argues that there is not one truth but many truths, none of which is or should be privileged (Flax 1987; Abbott et al. 2005). What we do support is a position that recognizes the importance of difference and yet acknowledges the significance of each of the multiple identities that individuals occupy. From this perspective it is possible to argue for a standpoints rather than a standpoint position. By doing this we acknowledge that gender, age, disability and so on are 'difference[s] that make a difference' but are not the only defining feature in anyone's life (Di Stephano 1990: 78).

This viewpoint supports our extending social research approach in several ways. First, it does not privilege the perspective of one group rather than another but acknowledges the significance of sameness and difference across and between groups of individuals. To explain this more simply we draw on Stanley and Wise's (1993: 21–2) argument that a feminist standpoints approach is useful in explaining women's lives because 'woman' can be argued to be a 'socially and politically constructed category, the ontological basis of which lies in a set of experiences rooted in the material world' and yet 'the experience of "women" is ontologically fractured and complex because we do not all share one single and unseamed reality'. Just as there are things that women share but things that divide women as a group there are views, experiences and material circumstances that divide older people, victims of crime, workers for voluntary organizations and so on and so on. Second, in adopting a stand-points approach we are not claiming to be searching for and finding the one and only truth but are acknowledging that the knowledge claims we do make are affected by time, place and personhood (of all involved) and are thus 'situated'. Third, this is an approach that does not make a claim for objectivity and/or value-freedom but rather recognizes that the personal is both political and theoretical and thus identifies the research process and product(s) as political.

'Insiders' and 'outsiders'

A fundamental question relevant to any research project is 'who is it for?' In relation to academic research all researchers, even those attracted to policy- and practice-orientated research and writing for political (as well as pragmatic) reasons, are motivated by issues of personal and institutional ambition (see Chapter 2). We acknowledge then, for example, that our involvement in the production of this book is not purely altruistic. In addition it is important to remind ourselves that our recognition of and commitment to the political aspects of the (in this case extended) research process does not automatically provide us with an 'insider' status. As academics and as researchers we (usually) remain 'strangers' to the people that we research; in advocating an extended research process we are not so naïve as to imply that we never leave the field or respondent group, move on to the next project or the next job. Indeed, it is our status as 'stranger' that sometimes makes it easier to complete the process and influence the product(s) of research. Georg Simmel (Wolff 1950) describes the stranger as a wanderer, the person who comes but eventually goes, the person who is perceived as being unlikely to censure confidences and unlikely to gossip to the rest of the group. On the other hand when respondents (and funders/commissioners) have or perceive they have a connection with us this may be the time that they tell us the secret that nobody else knows, feel confidence to ask us for or give us advice (e.g. Cotterill and Letherby 1994;

Collins 1998). Our status then as 'outsider' or 'insider' (recognizing of course that we can be both at the same time) brings with it further responsibility in terms of research ethics.

Social research is a dynamic social and human process that often involves an intrusion into people's lives. Researchers have a responsibility to their respondents and need to ensure that the design, process and delivery of the product(s) of research are ethical and not exploitative. But defining 'ethics' is itself a complicated process. Universities and professional organizations produce ethical guidelines for researchers and increasingly researchers have to present reports on their method and approach to internal and external ethics committees. Thus, there is no single set of ethical rules or prescriptions. In addition there is evidence to suggest that the issues that are of concern to 'ethics committees' may be different to those of concern to funders, commissioners and respondents (see Truman 2003 and Chapter 5 for further discussion).

It is possible to argue that if respondents freely agree to be part of research then they have some responsibility for the relationship and it is important to note that power is a two-way process and researchers do not always hold the balance of power both in terms of their relationships with funders and commissioners and with respondents. It is important not to over-passify research respondents, not least by assuming that they are always vulnerable within research. Some respondents do not feel disempowered by either their life experience or by the research relationship and it may be patronizing of the researcher to assume that the respondent needs to be empowered by the process. Also, research relationships are fluid and jointly constructed and at times during the research process it is the researcher that might feel vulnerable and/or at a disadvantage. This may be the case when researching individuals who are older, more experienced, more knowledgeable and/or when undertaking research with people with sexist, racist, homophobic (and so on) views and attitudes (e.g. Cotterill 1992; Ramsay 1996; Collins 1998). In addition to the emotional danger suggested here it is important also to acknowledge that research can subject researchers to physical danger (Lee-Treweek and Linkogle 2000).

Yet, within research it is usually the researchers who have the time, resources and skills to conduct methodological work, to make sense of experience and locate individuals in historical and social contexts. The researcher usually has control over, for example, the construction of the questionnaire, the order in which the questions are asked in a qualitative interview, the frequency and timing of visits to a research site and, as noted above, the associated status that this brings. Furthermore, researchers who study people who are (arguably) particularly vulnerable (e.g. children, intellectually disabled adults) and who undertake covert research – that does not take place with the knowledge of those being studied – need to think even more carefully about the possible exploitative aspects of the research process (for further discussion of these issues see, for example, Kelly et al 1994; Barnes and Mercer 1997; Hood et al 1999; Thomas and O'Kane 1999; Humphries 2000a).

One response to the suggestion that researchers are unable to achieve empathy with, and therefore fully represent, people who are not like them is to argue that researchers should not aim to represent the 'other'. This, the argument goes, not only prevents misrepresentation but also limits the possibilities of exploitation. Not least because, as Sue Wilkinson and Celia Kitzinger suggest (1996: 13 drawing on the work of Olson and Shopes), there is a 'temptation to exaggerate the exotic, the heroic, or the tragic aspects of the lives of people with little power'. However, there are problems here, not least because academia is not representative of all groups (in relation to gender, ethnicity, age, dis/ability and so on). Thus, if researchers do not undertake research on individuals and groups unlike themselves the experience of some remains unconsidered. It also implies that minority groups cannot research and represent majority groups which in turn implies that criticism of the more powerful is inappropriate (Wilkinson and Kitzinger 1996; Letherby 2003a).

Ethical issues are of course not just relevant in terms of the collection of data. It is the researcher who is more often than not responsible for the final analysis and presentation of the data. Thus, researchers 'take away the words' of respondents and have the power of editorship. Also, although researchers – through their own reflexive practice and adherence to ethical guidelines – may collect the data in an ethically sound, non-exploitative way, the way the findings are used (which is not always within the researchers' control) may still negatively affect respondents. This final point is of course a further argument for extending social research but even within this approach it is likely that it is the researchers and not the respondents (and others who will likely be affected by the research) who will more often than not hold the balance of power throughout the research and have control of both the material and authoritative resources. With all of this in mind Judith Stacey (1991: 144) argues that 'elements of inequality, exploitation, and even betrayal are endemic to [research]'.

This leads some to argue that researchers should be aware of the power that they hold and should make themselves vulnerable and try and 'equalize' their relationships with respondents which would allow for 'empowerment' through research (e.g. Stanley and Wise 1993). This may involve including respondents in the construction of the research design, investment of the researchers' self and life experience in research encounters, involving respondents in the checking of data before the presentation of the research report and working with respondents and/or commissioners on research outputs and outcomes (see Chapters 5–8). However, when aiming for an emancipatory research process it is an illusion to think that, in anything short of a fully participatory research project – or a user controlled project (Turner and Beresford 2005), respondents can have anything approaching 'equal' knowledge (about what is going on) to the researcher. It may also be simplistic to assume that an approach which includes the respondents at all levels is ultimately empowering for respondents. As Diane Wolf (1996: 26) notes, so-called 'participatory' research 'can entail very disparate levels of input from research subjects' and respondents may not wish this type of involvement. So, there may be a tension between the desire to 'give respondents a voice' and the making of knowledge, not least because individuals may not necessarily possess the knowledge (or have the desire) to explain everything about their lives. Or, involving respondents in development work following the production of a research report may not be what they themselves want. Arguably, equal-izing relationships within research could also be seen to be exploitative in that it could encourage isolated individuals to come forward and reveal aspects of their experience that they later regret (Finch 1984; Cotterill 1992). Furthermore, making people feel powerful within the extended research pro-cess does not necessarily change the emotional and material circumstances of their lives.

Analysis and re/presentation

In addition to the traditional 'scientific' approaches being challenged for their focus on theory testing and claim for value-neutrality and value-freedom, they have also been challenged for claiming that the research process is linear and objective – 'hygienic' in fact (Stanley and Wise 1993; Kelly *et al.* 1994). As this book demonstrates, an extending social research approach is anything but hygienic and must allow for changes in direction, revisions to procedure and process and new innovation. This may seem to suggest that a qualitative grounded approach to data collection is more appropriate. It is true that this approach supports that known as Grounded Theory (Strauss and Corbin 1990) as the researcher does not begin with a theory and then prove it but allows the relevant theory to emerge from the data and is concerned to locate theory in respondents' worlds and the desire to reject abstract theory. However, as others have noted, grounded theory implies complete induction and that work is free of political influence (Stanley and Wise 1990; Maynard 1994; Morley 1996). But, as Liz Stanley and Sue Wise (1990: 22) argue: 'researchers do not have "empty heads" and therefore it is imperative to acknowledge the gendered, classed, racial and so on intellectual and physical presence of the researcher'. We agree with this and add that we must also acknowledge the gendered, classed, racial and so on intellectual and physical *and emotional* presence of all of those involved. Involving respondents and/or commissioners in the analysis stage of a project not only challenges traditional so-called 'hygienic' approaches but also more so-called radical approaches. Thus, we are not sug-gesting that some methods rather than others are more appropriate to our suggested extending social research model, but rather that all types of social science research need to pay attention to research outputs and outcomes within/during the research process.

End points

In this chapter we have attempted to outline the significance of our extending social research approach to knowledge and knowledge production. Thus, we have been concerned with the relationship between extending social research and epistemology. Some might ask 'why bother?' Liz Kelly *et al.* (1994: 32), writing about a similar debate within feminism, criticize what they call the 'romance with epistemology' and argue that less concern should be given to 'women's ways of knowing' and more to 'discover[ing] and understand[ing] what is happening in women's lives, and how we might change it'. Similarly Ann Oakley (2004: 194) (although part of the epistemological debate herself) argues that what we should concern ourselves with most is 'the extent to which our work resonates with the experiences and needs of people outside the academic world'. We certainly agree with Kelly and her colleagues and with Oakley that our best research contributes a positive difference to people's lives, rather than merely becoming part of academic debate. But as one of us has suggested elsewhere, and we further argue here, 'knowing' and 'doing' are intertwined (see Letherby 2003a, 2004). The important point here then is a constant critical and self-critical engagement with the (complete) research process and our place within it. We are not suggesting that 'a concern with the research process' should take 'precedence over what the *research is . . . about*', as Miriam Glucksmann also fears is sometimes happening (1994: 150, our emphasis), but we are suggesting that the research process is indeed part of, rather than a tool to uncover, what the *research is about*.

Notes

1. Feminists' insistence that not only is the 'personal political' but also theoretical has not just influenced what we study (e.g. intimacy and emotion as well as housework and human reproduction) but the way in which we study. Acceptance of the signifi- cance of the personal – both politically and theoretically – has led to the recognition of the value of reflexivity and emotion as a source of insight as well as an essential part of research. As Judith Okley (1992: 9) notes:

   This stands against an entrenched tradition which relegates the personal to the periphery and to the 'merely anecdotal'; pejoratively contrasted in positivistic social science with generalizable truth.

4

Extending social research: how?

Paul Bywaters and Gayle Letherby

Introduction • Enhancing impact throughout the research process
• End points

Introduction

As will be clear by now, the stance of this book is that all research is an intervention. You cannot embark on a piece of research or even prepare a proposal
without having an impact on other people and on the field of study. Of course,
the impact may be tiny or even negligible but even an unsuccessful bid for a
project proposing documentary analysis may have been read by reviewers or
discussed with colleagues and, in a small way perhaps, influenced their thinking and subsequent action. And the time taken in the preparation of any bid has
an opportunity cost in terms of the time not spent on other work which also
could have had an impact on others. Therefore, we believe that the only ethical
position for researchers is to consider what the impact of our work might be and
to act deliberately, consciously making the best informed choices we can about
how to act. Of course, our promotion of the extended social research model is
not based on this negative position of not being able to avoid research having
an impact but by our positive belief in gaining value from research.

While we are suggesting that it is unethical not to engage with issues to do with the impact of research, we are not implying that there is a single 'right' way to do so or simple blueprints for ethical action. Each research situation has to be examined in its own right and ethical principles applied alongside methodological and practical considerations. We are not advocating a single approach or method but proposing that a set of issues linked to the publication, application and implementation of research findings must be considered as integral to the research process.

This chapter is about choosing routes through that complex decision-making process. It is about *how* researchers can turn a commitment to viewing impact as a central responsibility of their work into practical actions. We recognize and draw on the growing literature about evidence-based practice and research utilization (e.g. NHS CRD 1999; Nutley 2003; Walter *et al.* 2004a) even though, in our view, that literature sometimes implies that the primary responsibility for translating research findings into practice rests beyond the research process itself, a position we take issue with. In doing so, we focus on the role of researchers in enhancing the impact of research in addition to, and in collaboration with, the efforts of policy makers, practitioners and others to make sense and use of research findings.

The literatures of evidence-based practice with its contested claims (Webb 2001; Gibbs and Gambill 2002) and research utilization also overlap with what, more commonly in the business world, is called 'knowledge transfer' (Argote and Ingram 2000), described and discussed on the ESRC website: (www.esrcsocietytoday.ac.uk/ESRCInfoCentre/Support/knowledge%5 Ftransfer/). There is some convergence in both these literatures with our argument, as the evidence on research utilization increasingly suggests that the involvement throughout the processes of research production of stakeholders who have an interest in research findings enhances the likelihood of action being taken based on the findings (Walter *et al.* 2004a). Many of the issues outlined here are picked up and explored further with practice examples in the subsequent four chapters.

As we discuss particularly in Chapters 5 and 6, we are proposing a much closer relationship between all stakeholders in the research process than is implied in much of the research methods literature, and a relationship that continues into implementation. The researcher–stakeholder relationship is a two-way process involving a change of perspective for many policy makers, managers, practitioners on the one hand and for many researchers on the other. Like Isabel Walter and colleagues (2004a), we argue for the development of these two-way relationships from the time of decisions to make funding available and the writing of proposals onwards – and for the involvement of the populations who will be affected by changed policies and practices. And we are arguing for researchers to be involved in processes of application and implementation, for researchers to engage in the practice world as well as letting the practice world become more influential in research decision-making processes. So when we discuss the impact of research, we are not just concerned with developing awareness of research – with communicating findings, but with changes in policy and in practice. For this, communication is a necessary but not a sufficient element (NHS CRD 1999).

The body of the chapter concerns the implications of our approach for the whole of the research process and outlines some of the key ways in which paying attention to impact has an influence throughout the research process. While not pretending that any of these activities are just functional exercises without complexity or contention, we discuss the practical implications of our approach as they affect:

- identifying research users;
- developing research ideas;
- design;
- contracting;
- access;
- fieldwork and analysis;
- writing/reporting/presenting findings;
- continuing engagement in research outcomes.

At each stage we consider the problems and barriers to be faced.

Enhancing impact throughout the research process

Identifying research users

A central issue for improving the impact of research findings is engagement with research users (Somekh *et al.* 2005) – what Huberman (1994) called 'sustained interactivity' (see Chapter 2). If end users are participants throughout the research process, their commitment to using the results is greater, the focus of the research and, therefore, the findings are more likely to be relevant to policy, practice and everyday concerns and they are more likely to be framed in a way that lends itself to application (Nutley 2003; Walter *et al.* 2004a).

Social researchers have been criticized by both governments and service users for failing to address their concerns adequately (Beresford and Evans 1999; Hughes 2003a). As we saw in Chapter 2, a common criticism of social research is that it fails to pass the test of relevance and utility. This is best addressed if research is conceived of as a collaborative activity between researchers and other stakeholders, whereas the model implicit in most research textbooks is that of the lone practitioner operating in a situation without financial constraints. As Sue Wilkinson and Celia Kitzinger (1996: 18) argue, it is important to remember that our work should not 'be so much about the other as the interplay between the researcher and the Other'. Extending social research includes the acknowledgement that the 'Other' in research includes funders and other stakeholders as well as respondents.

From the outset, whether that is the commissioning process or proposal development, researchers should consider who would potentially be involved in the process of undertaking research and who it is hoped will use the research findings. They should attempt to ensure that those organizations or individuals who may use the findings are aware of the knowledge that will be generated and are in the best possible position to make use of it. Walter *et al.* (2004a), from a social care perspective, describe the following as the key stakeholders, alongside researchers themselves, in research utilization:

- governance organizations;
- research funders;
- practitioners and managers;
- trainers and training providers;
- service users and service user groups;
- facilitators such as Making Research Count or the Social Care Institute for Excellence.

John Lavis and colleagues (2003) produce an overlapping list of audiences for knowledge transfer in health and health care:

- general public/service recipients;
- service providers;
- managerial decision makers;
- policy decision makers.

Researchers and funders, whoever is initiating the research activity, should develop strategies for reaching, influencing and building collaborative relationships with these groups and individuals from the initiation of research projects. A spin-off from paying attention to this is that it can help to sharpen the focus of the project itself. 'Who are the expected beneficiaries of this work?', and 'How are they going to be influenced to bring about change through this research?' are valuable questions to consider at the outset. For example, the Centre for Social Justice (CSJ) has frequently been asked to undertake evaluations of pilot social care and health services when they have only a few months left to run. Managers remember that evaluation was a condition of the original funding bid and realize that they are about to be asked to report to the programme funder. While it may sometimes be appropriate to offer assistance, such post-hoc evaluations are too late to help projects to maximize the development of the service through interim findings, rarely tell project managers much that they did not know and usually cannot be effectively carried out because of the absence of baseline data. This undermines the chances of influencing service provision more generally because of the poor quality evidence about the effectiveness of the pilot and because there is also rarely significant funding available for communication and development or a recognition of the lead time required for service change if the pilot service is to be rolled out more widely. Often such evaluation is more concerned with auditing the use of public funds – was the money spent on what it was given for? – rather than on the more important questions of whether it made a significant difference and whether lessons can be learnt for future and wider service development. Applying the extending social research model means that we try to clarify with funders/commissioners what they are expecting to achieve from an evaluation done at this stage and negotiate with them about whether their expectations can be met. Sometimes such contracts will have to be refused or, alternatively, they may be seen as a point of entry to a longer research relationship with the funder, in which we would try to influence the setting up of evaluation processes in subsequent projects.

Developing research ideas

Involving stakeholders such as service provider organizations, policy makers in local or national government departments or service representatives in the development of research ideas and programmes does not guarantee that research findings will be put to greater use at the end of the process but it does increase the chances that this will be the case. As well as sometimes facilitating access to research respondents, stakeholder involvement in developing research ideas can:

- improve the likelihood that research will fit the priorities of practitioners, managers, policy makers or service users;
- enable stakeholders to shape aspects of the research agenda to meet their organizational or group needs better;
- increase stakeholders' sense of ownership of the process and therefore their commitment to using the findings.

This involvement in developing ideas can take at least three main forms. First, involvement can start with stakeholders. The idea can be theirs and they can engage with researchers to refine and carry out the work. For example, the CSJ was recently asked to undertake an assessment of access to health services by black and minority ethnic groups in a local town. The project resulted from a long consultation between the Primary Care Trust and members of local community organizations. Second, researchers and stakeholders can work in partnership, developing ideas together by creating a jointly owned research agenda. This is exemplified in the later 'Young Parents' projects described in Chapter 5. Third, researchers can consult with stakeholders about an idea they have developed and modify the direction and content of the work in the light of feedback. This was reflected in the development of a project on the role of gardens and gardening in older people's lives, in which, first, Age Concern and subsequently older people themselves were consulted about the development of our ideas.

These kinds of partnership processes in developing research ideas are increasingly built into funders' expectations. For example, the Joseph Rowntree Foundation (JRF) often requires research proposals to demonstrate clear evidence of research partnerships having been established between researchers and service-providing organizations as well as with representatives of service users. Research programmes at JRF are also developed and approved in committees on which policy-making and practice organizations are represented. Increasingly, service-provider organizations, whether from the public, commercial or independent sectors, are realizing the power they have to permit or refuse access to researchers and are using this to exert greater influence or control over research agendas. Research governance systems, particularly those developed by the Department of Health for health-related research (and by extension for social care organizations), through Research Ethics Committees (RECs) and local R & D Committees (DoH 2005), effectively allow service providers to determine what research can and cannot take place. These and other factors are tilting the balance of power in favour of provider, policy-making and service-user organizations. They require researchers to engage with such stakeholders from the earliest stages of research processes if empirical research is going to be carried out at all, not just to maximize the impact that the implementation of findings may achieve.

There are risks in the development of such close relationships and in the shift in power towards policy makers and providers. For example, the UK government is taking an increasingly close grip on research funding processes through its control of the Research Councils.

> The Delivery Plans are part of a comprehensive Performance Management Framework which will enable OST to demonstrate the contribution that each Research Council is making towards achieving government targets. This Framework includes a series of performance metrics (the 'Outputs Framework') and a set of targets and milestones arising from the activities set out in the Delivery Plan (the 'Scorecard').
>
> (ESRC 2005b)

This control of the research agenda can be used to exclude examination of sensitive or unpopular issues, eroding the independence of researchers. Understandably, governments may be unlikely to fund their critics. Current government policy for research (HM Treasury 2004: 6) makes clear that it expects publicly funded research to be more responsive to the needs of the economy and public services:

- Research Councils' programmes to be more strongly influenced by and delivered in partnership with end users of research.
- Continue to improve UK performance in knowledge transfer and commercialisation from universities and public labs towards world leading benchmarks.

This can be repeated at the local level, where, for example, the NHS control of access by researchers to staff or patients through local RECs may prevent research being conducted that is expected to be highly critical of the policy or practice of the NHS and can exclude research that challenges medical research paradigms (see also Chapter 2).

The increasing expectation from UK government acting through the higher education funding councils that every effort will be made to commercialize academic research and to charge what is considered the full economic cost, with overhead charges calculated as above 100 per cent, is a further barrier to constructive partnerships. This ethos works against collaborative relationships between researchers and other stakeholders, except where both perceive common commercial interest, and does not encourage transparency, for example with regard to cost, which is a necessary element for creating trust.

The idea that knowledge transfer should have a financial value protected by intellectual property rights is being challenged by the open access movement which has gained significant institutional support, for example from the International Federation of Library Associations and Institutions, (www.ifla. org/V/press/oa240204.html):

> By 'open access' to this literature, . . . we mean its free availability on the public internet, permitting any users to read, download, copy, distribute, print, search, or link to the full texts of these articles, trawl them for indexing, pass them as data to software, or use them for any other lawful purpose, without financial, legal, or technical barriers other than those inseparable from gaining access to the internet itself. The only constraint on reproduction and distribution, and the only role for copyright in this domain, should be to give authors control over the integrity of their work and the right to be properly acknowledged and cited.
>
> (Open Society Institute 2005: 4)

Some kinds of research funding and research institutions might be reluctant to join with partners who had a commitment to open access while, on the other hand, it is likely that new social movements might expect such a stance. These conflicts are, of course, not caused by attempts to build partnerships in developing research ideas but by the context in which research operates.

Design

More positively, the effective and detailed consideration of outputs and outcomes embedded in the design of research proposals may well (and, arguably, should) help a funding bid to succeed. The ESRC's 'new mission places emphasis on ensuring that researchers engage as fully as possible with the users of research outcomes' (ESRC 2005c). Most UK and non-UK major funders expect that an account of how 'dissemination' will occur will be part of any proposal and an explanation of how the outputs of research will lead to practical outcomes is likely to become increasingly significant in funding decisions. The distinction was made in a recent UK Department of Health and Kings College, London research policy paper (2006) that research should be seen as a three-stage process in which the second and third stages are dissemination and impact.

It is too late to consider these issues when the end stage of research is reached. The ESRC Guidance rightly recommends that researchers 'build dissemination activities into the structure of your research plan rather than give them passing reference as an after thought at the end' (ESRC 2005c). As we have already argued, building research relationships with stakeholders enhances ownership and the likelihood of action. Building such relationships takes time and ideally takes place throughout the research process. For example, having an Advisory Committee or Steering Group (see Chapter 6) can be valuable in promoting the findings of research but again the time and costs involved have to be designed into the research proposal. Similarly, a well-developed media strategy cannot easily be put together as findings are produced but requires the careful targeting of key media outlets, the building of relationships with journalists, the planned production of appropriate materials, perhaps the setting up of a national conference and so on (ESRC 2001).

The ESRC assessment framework has four criteria, which include 'Communication Strategy and Planned Outputs' (ESRC 2005d). The application form for Research Grants requires applicants to outline the 'potential impacts of the research' and their 'user engagement and communication plans'. However, for the ESRC, as for other funders, the focus is on communication or 'dissemination' and potential impacts and not on the more extensive (and expensive) change-oriented tasks of application and implementation. Those writing proposals for the ESRC are asked to indicate how their work may have an impact but not what they will do to ensure that it has a greater chance of doing so.

Moreover, it is uncertain just how influential such criteria are in the final decisions on funding alongside criteria covering methodology or subject matter, or whether funders are sufficiently aware of the costs involved in comprehensive publication, application and implementation strategies. However, for us, it is clear that a research design driven by the intention of producing change must give adequate weight and resources to the production of outputs and outcomes and this must be written into research contracts.

Contracts

Contracts outlining the terms and conditions under which research funding is granted conventionally cover the rights of academics to publish articles in academic journals and other outlets. Such contracts can provoke useful discussions between researchers, funders and other stakeholders about the sometimes contentious issues of authorship, ownership, intellectual property rights, whether material for publication must be vetted and so on. Contracts will often outline what funders expect in the way of research reports and sometimes will require researchers' participation in a national conference or a series of workshops. However, often the elements to do with publication, application and implementation are left vague, or again seen as something which will occur after the research is completed, with a greater focus being placed on the production of research than its impact.

Leaving such elements unclear is particularly unhelpful when the outcomes of research are or can be seen as negative for the funder. A service or project being evaluated may be found to be ineffective or costly or to have unexpected negative side effects. The research may reveal unpalatable evidence about the internal workings of the organization which has funded and/or hosted the research (see the institutional racism example in Chapter 6). Sometimes, research will be picked up by a salacious media acting on common stereotypes, as Nina Hallowell and colleagues (2005) found out. Such possible or potential outcomes should be considered in advance so that stakeholders are aware and strategies considered. Not all such strategies will be written into contracts, of course, but ways of handling difficulties between the researchers and stake-holders are best discussed before they happen. In another of the CSJ's projects, a local authority commissioned a study of its child care services, primarily a project led by a voluntary sector organization. However, the results included evidence of weaknesses in the local authority's policies and practices. It had been agreed that the draft report would be read and commented on by the local authority before it was made public, even internally. However, there was no agreement about how long the local authority would have to make its comments and a delay of several months was just one of the tactics used to avoid negative criticism. A time limit and other limits on the control the local authority could exercise over the report could have been written into the research contract, although whether this would have made the authority any more likely to publish and implement the findings is a different question. Indeed, raising such issues early in a research relationship could imply – or create – a lack of trust.

Access

Persuading gatekeepers to allow access and respondents to take part in research depends in part on convincing both parties of the value of giving their time and, sometimes, other resources. Being clear about how the research will be of benefit to the objectives of their organizations, to themselves or to other people like them can be an effective as well as an ethical strategy. Benefits do not necessarily have to be direct for the respondents individually, although rewarding the expertise, knowledge and time of respondents may well be appropriate, as recent UK government guidance indicates (DoH 2006). This can be a complex issue where respondents are not in employment and their social security benefits may be affected.

Another major issue with respondents who are in receipt of care or other services may be whether their involvement will affect their entitlements or the services they receive in any way, positively or negatively. Our research with asylum seekers and refugees has made particularly apparent the vulnerability that respondents may feel if they are implicitly or explicitly asked to criticize, through research, services that they rely on in their everyday lives. But in the CSJ's projects, we have also found that a common motivation amongst respondents is altruism: the thought that their participation would have beneficial effects for others. This often means that they want to know that the research will produce change for others, if not for themselves, and researchers arranging access with respondents and asking for informed consent should consider how they can reassure respondents on this issue alongside the more conventional concerns (of researchers and ethics committees (see also Chapter 5)) about confidentiality and risk.

Fieldwork and analysis

A number of aspects of the fieldwork stage of research can have a bearing on the outputs and outcomes of research, and not just through the findings that are generated. While gathering data there are often extensive contacts with potential research users as well as with respondents. The nature and quality of these contacts can have a significant influence on how the subsequent research findings are received by those immediately involved in the research. If the focus of the research is the organization that is also the location of the fieldwork then all the contacts with staff in the organization will affect their response to the findings. The research process affects how the findings are received, interpreted and acted on by those who have been involved. This is not only a matter of creating collaborative relationships, as we discussed earlier, but also a matter of developing trust in the researchers' skills and values. It is easier to hear and harder to dismiss messages from people who are liked and trusted than from those who are seen as distant, unsympathetic or unprofessional.

Intelligence about how an organization operates which comes from contacts with staff during the research process is also valuable. For example, it may subsequently be applied in producing recommendations and in ensuring that the research report is read by the people and considered in the forums which have the power to make the relevant decisions. If recommendations are made without knowledge of what may be possible, they are likely to be ignored.

As we have already suggested, developing close relationships between researchers and staff in the research location can also have risks, as researchers can never divest themselves entirely of personal feelings and prejudices when gathering and interpreting evidence. Putting it crudely, positive relationships may make the researchers reluctant to give 'bad news'. However, distant or even conflictual relationships may lead to fundamental disputes about the interpretation of data and barriers may be placed in the way of completing the research. As argued in Chapter 3, the traditional assumption that independence and distance between researcher and researched leads to a valuable objectivity is an unreal and unethical model, what Bridget Somekh and Cathy Lewin (2005: 65) describe as 'a naïve epistemology', obscuring the allegiances and persona of the researcher.

A direct way of engaging with 'host' organizations is to report back on data being collected during the processes of fieldwork and analysis rather than just at the end (Hughes 2003a, see especially Chapter 2). The issue of when and to whom feedback is given during the fieldwork stage of the research process is bound up with the researchers' perspectives about the nature and ownership of knowledge generated in the research process. Even in the absence of an explicit 'action research' model we would argue that it is rarely possible to gather data in a hermetically sealed manner, uninfluenced by the process. However, giving feedback during the research process can have a variety of benefits for the research process. It can help researchers to check the accuracy of their understanding of the data they have gathered and thereby will assist with issues of validity and analysis. In terms of the impact of the research, giving feedback during the research process is likely to help to keep funders or service providers involved with and interested in the research findings. The time scales for research are sometimes slower than practitioners and managers operate on; they want results more quickly, and providing early feedback can contribute to an early search for service improvements. The dialogue created with service providers or other host organizations can also help to shape the information collected later in the research project and avoid the research taking directions that do not meet the objectives of the funders (Noffke and Somekh 2005).

Some will view feeding back during the process of data gathering as potentially contaminating the results, for example, allowing service providers to alter their policies or practices during the process thereby making the evaluation of a service more complex or perhaps risking premature changes before results are sufficiently robust. It can also be the case that preliminary findings get acted on only for later results to suggest different conclusions. The first reported data is likely to have the greatest impact. Researchers making interim reports need to think carefully about what data to report, when and with what accompanying warnings. However, a rigid attempt to remain silent about findings until research is complete can raise ethical questions, especially where harm might be occurring or where services wish to be responsive to user perspectives. An open dialogue which involves discussion of these issues in advance or of the limitations of interim results can be the way to negotiate these complexities.

Writing/reporting/presenting

How to 'write up' research is widely discussed in the research methods literature. Both Darlington and Scott (2002) and Letherby (2003a) list and discuss some of the authors who have tackled this topic. But it has long been recognized that there is no necessary relationship between reporting research and changes in practices and policies affecting people's lives (Huberman 1994; NHS CRD 1999). So, for us, the task of writing up and reporting research is only in part a technical issue of representing findings effectively; more importantly it involves strategic decisions designed to maximize the impact of the findings (ESRC 2006a).

As far as writing up is concerned, the extension of the research process involves researchers determining (or at least planning) strategies to be adopted for communicating research findings at the outset of the project design. This is discussed in greater detail in Chapter 7. Key questions to ask in determining the writing/reporting strategy include:

- What is the purpose of the strategy?
- Who are the target audiences?
- What outlets should you target?
- Which methods and media can you employ to communicate the messages?

Necessarily, these questions will be bounded by issues of time and cost that have to be considered when funding proposals are being made and projects planned. Of course, like all plans, a communications strategy will be subject to subsequent influences, both within and external to the research process. These will include the nature and significance of the findings, which cannot be entirely known in advance, and the academic, professional and public environment at the time when findings are available. Your work may be ready at a moment when it is highly topical or alternatively have faded from current agendas. This will affect the opportunities available for communicating the research messages.

By starting with the purpose of the strategy, the researcher is asked to consider fundamental questions often ignored in the methods literature. The aim may be to inform or to provoke discussion, to meet the expectations of the funder or stakeholder organizations, or directly to bring about changes in policy and practice. Often an unspoken element in the process is to advance the career of the researcher or the status and reputation of a research group. Clarity about the aims of communication is helpful in deciding the answers to the other strategic questions. Different aims may apply in different circumstances and at different stages of the research process. For example, Clarissa White and colleagues (2003) have produced a useful classification of kinds of outputs as:

- developmental;
- summary;
- selective;
- comprehensive.

The developmental presentation or report is best suited to promote debate and discussion based on early findings or analysis. It is likely to take place while analysis is still continuing. A comprehensive report cannot be completed until the late stages of the project, when all the fieldwork and analysis is considered to have been completed. Of course, subsequent feedback is always, in effect, new data. It is also an error to think that you have to reproduce all the findings for all audiences. Again the primary issues in being selective are the purpose of the communication and the target audience or audiences.

Christina Hughes (2003b: 3) and her colleague Arwen Raddon (2001) also suggest a number of diverse strategies for reporting findings. In addition to the traditional and non-traditional forms of publishing and interim reports during the process of research, they include publicizing findings through education and training programmes and using networks, often electronically based, of practitioners, academics and policy makers. Again the purpose of the strategy is important. If you want to influence professional practice then building research findings into education and training programmes and establishing them as part of standard curricula may be a key method, working through networks designed to ensure that research findings reach and influence practitioners and managers such as Making Research Count and Research In Practice. But neither education and training nor professional networks will reach a wider 'lay' audience, who are more likely to pick up information through the TV, radio, magazines or newspapers or the internet. If the purpose is to create a more informed public and to strengthen lay knowledge, researchers have to engage more effectively than we often have in the past with more widely available media outlets.

Academics have often been accused (Huberman 1994) of insularity, of speaking to their own community with a focus on the advancement of knowledge rather than communicating effectively to research users, including the public. The rapid development of electronic media in the past twenty years has increasingly undermined any excuses for such a stance with websites and email lists, in particular, creating low-cost opportunities for making findings widely available. This was brought home very powerfully to one of the authors when over 50,000 copies of a research report and set of associated guidance leaflets resulting from a project on self-harm (Bywaters and Rolfe 2002) were downloaded within a year of publication, a far larger audience than would ever have been reached through academic publications (see Chapter 7 for further detail).

Another accusation that could be levelled about academics' approaches to the publication of findings is a lack of creative imagination or of communication skills in publicizing their work. There is a very limited literature on the use of a variety of forms of the arts to publish and communicate findings (Rosenstein 2002). But from our experience and conversations with other researchers and from our observation of the presentation of research papers at conferences there is an increasing use of drama, video/DVD, posters, photographs and other media to get the messages across. It is also often the case that publications and presentations are only in English but, again, there is an increasing demand for work to be presented in accessible ways to a variety of audiences. This either requires that academics develop new skills themselves or that they develop new partnerships with people who have the skills.

All universities will have press offices that should be able to assist researchers to publicize their work but from our experience the quality of this support is variable. Many of the large service provider funders, such as local authorities, primary care trusts and voluntary organizations will also have press and marketing departments and researchers who work in these settings or in collaborative partnerships with these organizations should make use of their expertise. The skills that these specialists have to offer can be invaluable in producing attractive, well-targeted outputs and planning and executing public campaigns. It is never too early in a project's life to make a first approach about collaborative publicity. The Society Today website (ESRC 2006b) has an extensive range of guidance on making best use of the media to maximize impact on policy making.

Continuing engagement

Writing and reporting research, producing *outputs*, is only one element in the process of trying to ensure that research findings have useful *outcomes*. As we explore in more depth in Chapter 8, extending the research role to include involvement in the processes of application and implementation of findings can have benefits for both research users and researchers.

For research users, there is an opportunity to gain maximum benefit from the expertise of researchers. One aspect of this could be that researchers – as outsiders and 'experts' – may have a particular credibility with staff that insiders may lack. The NHS CRD (1999) evidence-based report on getting research into practice concluded that professional behaviours are most likely to be influenced by multi-method, multifaceted interventions. And, of course, influencing professional behaviours is only one way of producing change through research.

For researchers, there is both satisfaction to be had in seeing first-hand that research can have a significant impact and feedback to be gained about the validity and value of the research findings. By continuing their engagement, researchers can be involved in piloting and evaluating changes in practice and policy resulting from their work. In doing so, they can also gain information which feeds back into the research findings. '[T]he validation of action research outcomes involves testing them out as the basis for new actions to see if the expected improvement results' (Noffke and Somekh 2005: 91).

Walter *et al.* (2004a: 52) suggest that there are three models for ways in which the research/practice relationship is enacted: the researcher-practitioner, embedded research and organizational excellence models. In the research-based practitioner model,

staff . . . take personal responsibility for research use; in the embedded model it is the manager's role to ensure that service delivery is informed by research. In the organisational excellence model the manager's task includes the local adaptation of existing research, commissioning local research and the establishment of ongoing development and evaluation activities.

However, these three models are not mutually exclusive. For researchers, understanding which models or models apply in the organizations for which findings are relevant can help to tailor their approach to maximize the effectiveness of their recommendations. For example, is the target population trainers, practitioners, policy writers or managers?

Extending the research role to include application goes beyond the process of simply writing recommendations through a collaborative process involving practitioners, managers, service users and other stakeholders (see above), although this itself is a skilful process requiring knowledge of the context in which the recommendations are to be applied. The process of application includes clarifying the messages arising from the research and integrating this evidence with relevant practice expertise and service user knowledge. A specific contribution that researchers can play in these processes is critically comparing messages emerging from their research to findings from other studies to provide a strengthened evidence base for policy and practice changes.

In our view, researchers should aim to ensure that wherever possible service users, or the public who are affected by policy and practice developments, are involved in these processes of application and implementation alongside employed staff in relevant organizations. Respondents may also wish to be involved in such discussions as their participation is frequently motivated by a desire to promote improvements in the circumstances of and services for others, if not for themselves.

Researcher involvement in implementation is most likely when the researcher is employed by the research user organization, perhaps as a researcher-practitioner, or when research has been carried out as part of continuing professional development. However, external researchers may also take on a variety of roles in implementation, for example as members of stakeholder Boards or Committees such as the various inter-agency Partnership Boards widely being employed in local government in the UK at the present time. Alternatively, researchers may continue and develop their involvement through contracts to deliver training or training materials or as consultants to a particular change process. These extended applied research roles, as we have suggested throughout this chapter, require additional skills and knowledge, for example knowledge of processes of organizational change. This degree of continuing involvement will not be requested or appropriate in all situations, but can be mutually beneficial. In our experience, as we shall discuss in more depth in Section 3 of the book, a longer term research partnership between researchers and service providers can result in a series or cycle of projects successively exploring questions that are revealed or remain unanswered by earlier projects and that progressively result in service improvements.

End points

As should now be clear, our extended research model implies an approach that affects every stage of the research process and adds new ethical consider-ations, new thought processes, new tasks and new skills. Our experience is that researchers – in practice – often already act in ways which go substantially beyond the processes described in research texts. There is a significant and growing pressure, worldwide, from research users and research funders (often one and the same or overlapping groups) for research to demonstrate its worth in terms of impact: on policy making, on services, on products, on efficiency or on profits. While research should not just be a response to whoever can pay the piper, two significant changes are required for this closer relationship between research and impact to be brought about. First, the training of researchers needs to change to involve a different conception of the research process and to teach different skills and draw on additional sources of know-ledge. Second, the organization and measurement of research needs to change to give greater recognition to impact. As Huw Davies *et al.* (2005) have argued, measures of research need to move beyond the mechanical focus on citations in other academic papers or the 'impact factor' measure of the prestige of journals to new ways of assessing what they describe as 'non-academic research impact'. In the UK, the 2008 Research Assessment Exercise, which will deter-mine the destination of major sources of research funding over many years, includes such impact as only one of a substantial number of indicators of so-called 'esteem', which itself only counts as a tiny proportion of the overall score given to the quality of research. Proposals to assess academic research in the UK after 2008 by a metrics-only system is unlikely to make non-academic research impact more central. Without the carrot that non-academic impact will directly advantage universities, the gap which the evidence-based prac-tice, research utilization and knowledge transfer 'industries' aim to fill is likely to continue to flourish.

Section 3

PROCESS AND PRODUCT: PRACTICE EXAMPLES

5

Setting the agenda

Zoebia Ali, Geraldine Brown, Paul Bywaters,
Dexter du Boulay, Maureen Hirsch,
Gayle Letherby and Helen Poole

*Introduction • Funding priorities and influences • Choosing a method or
methods • Ethics and ethical approval • Establishing research teams
• Intellectual property rights • Developing relationships: impact and
further research • End points*

Introduction

In this, the first of our four chapters concerned to demonstrate the process
of putting our extending social research approach into practice, we focus on
'setting the agenda'. Contrary to a step-by-step approach to the research process, we outline here the importance of thinking beyond the 'end' to the
potential impact of research on policy and practice from the moment a
research project is conceived. Currently many social researchers adopt methods
and approaches arising from principles of social justice and aim to allow individuals and groups both a voice and some control over the research process
and resultant product (see Hood *et al.* 1999; Beresford 2002; Letherby 2003a;
Turner and Beresford 2005; and Chapter 3). However, both research funded by
research councils (for example, the Economic and Social Research Council in
the UK or the Australian Research Council) and commissioned research pose
a number of dilemmas in this context, not least in the definition, design and

management of the research process, in the relationships between funders and commissioners and the relationships between researchers and researched[1] and others likely to be affected by the research outcomes. These dilemmas are relevant not just to setting the agenda but also to managing the whole process of research (which we consider in later chapters), although the significance of these issues has often been ignored both in the actual undertaking of, and in writings about, the beginnings of research.

In contrast to accounts which terminate the research process at 'writing up', in this chapter we reflect on the importance for our extending social research approach on how research projects are initiated. We begin with a consideration of funding priorities and influences as they relate to extending social research and then move on to the consequences of adopting an extending research approach for choosing a method or methods. Reflecting on ethics and ethical approval, on the establishment of research teams and determining intellectual property rights are also part of the creation of a research project and we consider these issues here as well. Towards the end of this chapter, we begin to look at developing relationships within research – an area on which we continue to focus throughout the rest of this book. We do not address these issues in the abstract but instead discuss our ideas through an analysis of a series of projects undertaken by a team of researchers from the Centre for Social Justice (CSJ) at Coventry University. Thus, our primary research example in this chapter is a series of past and ongoing projects on 'Young Parents', although we will refer additionally to other research examples. In terms of our key principles for extending social research, the specific aim of this chapter is to show how all stages are extended and that this requires rethinking the whole research process (principle 3) and to explore how researchers' skills are extended as they focus on the change process (principle 6) (see Chapter 1, p. 5, Table 1.1).

Funding priorities and influences

The role of different interests, for example on the Boards of Research Trusts, and wider agendas – such as government policy or the widespread emphasis on service user participation – can influence the agendas of public funding bodies. Thus, research funding does not appear out of thin air but is a political process itself, reflecting power relations in society. What funders and commissioners expect from researchers, in terms of making research findings public and maximizing the impact of the research on policy and practice audiences (both professional and lay), is also an increasing focus of political attention, as we have indicated previously (see Chapter 2). Consequently, these are issues which researchers have to consider from the outset of research (for example, when writing the proposal to apply for funding or in response to a tender) through to the application and implementation of the research findings. In general, proposals or bids are only successful if they meet the funders' priorities and are usually judged on research potential in terms of contribution to knowledge, general interest, theoretical developments, relevance to policy or practice initiatives and value for money (Genn 2004). The emphasis will vary, of course, according to the funder.

Increasingly, research funding councils and the major charitable research funders are requiring that bids to open calls for proposals or responses to research programmes include more or less detailed accounts of how findings are going to be made known. The dynamics and tensions are different when research is commissioned by service providers or business interests in that the commissioner may already have a view on how the findings may be used. This may affect the autonomy of the researcher(s). Such commissioned research will usually be almost exclusively concerned with the benefits research is likely to bring to their direct business interests: to the effectiveness of their policies and practices, their public image, their efficiency and so on. They may be less interested in breadth of publication than in how their own organization will be informed.

In addition, tensions can arise if part of the research is likely to involve scrutiny of the policies and procedures of the commissioning body. The climate of consumerism and the very nature of the new public management agenda necessitates an organizational culture in which there is a greater responsiveness to consumer and client demand, a search for excellence and measurable outcomes, and in which research and analysis are tools in this process (Massey and Pyper 2005). Another motivation for commissioners may be their own need to respond to government agendas.

These issues were relevant to Coventry NHS Trust (now Coventry Primary Care Trust) when in 2001 they put out to tender a project specification focusing on the housing needs of young parents in Coventry. This project, which members of the Centre for Social Justice tendered for and won, was commissioned as part of the local work relating to the national Teenage Pregnancy Strategy (SEU 1999).

The National Teenage Pregnancy Strategy was set out in the Social Exclusion Unit report on Teenage Pregnancy and involved a joint Department of Health and Department for Education and Skills Public Service Agreement. Arguably, although Lisa Arai (2003) highlights the difficulties in comparing statistics on teenage pregnancy with other European countries, Britain has the highest teenage pregnancy rate in Western Europe, with a rate double that of Germany, triple that of France and six times that of the Netherlands (SEU 1999). According to the Social Exclusion Unit report, each year 90,000 teenagers become pregnant and, of these, 7700 are under 16 and 2200 are under 14. The two national targets identified in the strategy were to:

- halve the under-18 conception rate in England by 2010 (with an interim reduction target of 15 per cent by 2003 included in the NHS Plan, which is also a Manifesto commitment); and

- increase the participation of teenage mothers in education, training or work to 60 per cent by 2010 to reduce the risk of long-term social exclusion.

As part of the second target of the strategy, which focused on supporting teenage parents and reducing their risk of long-term social exclusion, the aim was set that 'all lone parents under 18, who cannot live with their parents or partner, should be provided with suitable accommodation with support by 2003' (DoH 2002: 46). Furthermore, the *Government Response to the First Annual Report of the Independent Advisory Group on Teenage Pregnancy* (DoH 2002: 46) stated:

> The provision of good quality housing with support provides a springboard for the future for teenage parents and their children. Supported housing projects offer young parents adult and peer support to help prepare them for independent living, for example by helping to develop effective parenting and budget management skills. The projects also facilitate their return to education or employment, by brokering access to local colleges and training opportunities. Accommodation can range from hostels with twenty-four hour on-site support to clusters of independent flats or floating support where workers support young parents in existing housing stock across a wide area.

Coventry NHS Trust responded to the nationally set targets by appointing two Teenage Pregnancy Coordinators – one with a focus on prevention and one with a focus on support. A local Teenage Pregnancy Partnership Board (TPPB) was also established to oversee work in this area. In relation to housing, Coventry TPPB decided not to attempt to define in the abstract what young parents need and to provide it but first to try to find out what young people felt that they needed by asking them. Thus, they decided to commission research with the aim of collecting information about young pregnant women's and young mothers' experience of housing and their present and envisaged future housing needs.

This and subsequent projects have reflected both the research interests of members of the CSJ and both local and national policy and practice interests. The availability of funding for this research was directly the result of national policy implemented through local service providers. The intended outcomes, in policy and practice terms, were already set. This focus of the research was on gaining young women's views but as a precursor to taking action. The focus of 'writing up', in this instance, was on those who had the power to make decisions about future services. Both the intended outcomes and the key audience were reflected in our proposals about how the research would be reported and how it might make an impact.

Choosing a method or methods

When writing research bids or tenders researchers are required to detail the method or methods that they will use in the research, if successful in their application for funding. The relevance and significance of research findings and the use to which findings may be put are dependent on the appropriate choice of method, which must be designed to meet the aims and objectives of the project. But the methods should also be chosen with a view to generating the kind of evidence that would be most likely to produce a required impact in terms of both the funder and the prospective audience. Historically, quantitative methods have been more positively received as a result of the perception of quantitative methods as more rigorous, reliable and generalizable – more 'scientific' (see Chapter 3 for further discussion). But in recognition of the fact that a great deal of qualitative research and evaluation is also commissioned by the UK government, the National Centre for Social Research has produced a quality framework to set standards by which such work can be judged. This is deemed as a step towards ensuring that government policy is informed by robust, valid and appropriate research evidence. The framework is based around four guiding principles that research should be:

- *contributory* in advancing wider knowledge or understanding;
- *defensible in design* by providing a research strategy which can address the evaluation posed;
- *rigorous in conduct* through the systematic and transparent collection, analysis and interpretation of qualitative data;
- *credible in claim* through offering well-founded and plausible arguments about the significance of the data generated.

(Spencer *et al.* 2003)

It is, of course, important to challenge the view that qualitative research is somehow less valid, less reliable and less useful than quantitative research and it is important to choose appropriate methods to suit research programmes rather than research programmes being chosen to 'fit' favourite techniques (Kelly *et al.* 1994). As Ann Oakley (2004: 191) states: 'The most important criteria for choosing a particular research method is not its relationship to academic arguments about methods, but its fit with the question being asked in the research.' But prejudices still exist – both within and outside the academy – and those using qualitative methods may find they have to defend their case.

Qualitative methods are particularly appropriate when focusing on the experience of under-researched groups and/or groups that are misunderstood. With reference to teenage pregnancy Anne Phoenix suggests: 'The negative focus is produced by people who are not, themselves, "young mothers" but rather outsiders. There is generally a disjunction between "outsider" and "insider" perspectives' (1991: 86).

With this in mind we were encouraged by the initiative of Coventry TPPB to attempt to access the 'insider' perspective and were hopeful that our findings would influence policy. In our research bid we noted that one of the best ways to find out about people's feelings and experiences is to let them tell you about it themselves (Stanley and Wise 1983). So, if we won the research tender, we would collect the data though single and focus group interviews, which allow researchers to explore issues in greater depth than would be possible with larger groups (Gilbert 1993).

As Julianne Cheek (2000: 409) notes: 'funded qualitative [and quantitative] study puts a particular "spin" on the issues', influencing who assumes control of the research from its early stages of defining goals and objectives, progressing the research and sharing the outcomes. The researcher must trade a certain degree of autonomy for financial support and this is likely to cause tension when there are conflicting goals and expectations from funders, respondents and researchers. Clarifying expectations and setting ground rules before the research begins might seem pedantic but may help to avoid tensions within the working relationships later in the project.

Coventry TPPB were happy with our intended method so we had no problems of legitimacy here. There have been times, though, whilst undertaking subsequent 'Young Parents' projects (see below), when our approach has been valued less, not by the commissioners of our projects but by other individuals with more senior roles in the organization. In a later project, again on housing experience and need, for Warwickshire TPPB, the housing directors of the five regions of the county were concerned by our lack of statistics. Although in this report (Letherby *et al.* 2003) we detailed differential housing and social care needs across the country and highlighted significant problems with some of the current housing provision, the housing directors reacted to our report by stating that it did not provide them with the thing that they most wanted to know, which was 'how many young parents need accommodation each year'. Not only was this information almost impossible to collect, given inadequate counting mechanisms across the country, but identifying numbers is only part of the picture when aiming to understand young parents' housing needs. This experience highlights the problems that can occur when there is a disjunction between the expectations of commissioners, of researchers and other research stakeholders.

When clarifying expectations and ground rules there should also be reference to the composition of the respondent group, the intended outputs and outcomes beyond the traditionally defined research process and the role of the research team in producing these. We return to the issue of outputs and outcomes later in this chapter and in Chapters 7 and 8, but here focus a little more on respondent issues. There is a power dimension here in that senior and middle managers, while recognizing the need to elicit the views of staff and clients/consumers, are also motivated to demonstrate that they are performing effectively. So it is usually managers who commission research and subordinate staff and service users who are the 'subjects'[1] of such research. Anne Grinyer (1999), referring to Howard Becker (1967), elaborates this point. She notes that within organizations, there are superordinates (governing bodies or management) and subordinates (the work force or users of services). When conducting research within or for organizations, the latter are, more often than not, the 'subjects' of research commissioned by the former. Superordinates in any hierarchical structure are characterized by power, status, responsibility and accountability and alongside this there is often an expectation of deference to their views and perceptions. When scrutinizing issues of power and status it can be seen that, in many research projects, it is the superordinates who have the power and influence to identify and define the 'problem': that is, why the research is necessary and what its focus should be. This may create tension between management who are looking to have policies and practices vindicated and subordinates who challenge the functioning, efficiency or even *raison d'être* of the organization. Grinyer (1999) argues that the researcher role is quite different from that of a consultant who might be seen as the tool of management. Therefore, it is essential that commissioners are clear about the distinction between these two roles and that the researcher is clear about the boundaries of the research task.

Grinyer (1999) adds that commissioned research is overt by virtue of being commissioned by those with power and influence in the organization. However, from the point of view of the identified 'subjects' of the research, the subordinates and users of services, the research may be covert. When the behaviour and actions of those with power and status in an organization, who commission the research, come under scrutiny themselves as part of the process of social enquiry, problems may arise. Rarely do commissioners of research set out intending to be the 'subjects' of research, yet it would seem that the very nature of research within organizations implies the possibility that findings could relate to any part of the structure, functioning and operation of such organizations and, by implication, to individuals at all levels.

Again, although we recognize the validity of Grinyer's concern, this is not a problem that we have encountered to a great extent in our 'Young Parents' projects. That is not to say that there have been no tensions. In all of the projects we have undertaken in this area so far (see below for full list), we have collected data from professionals and practitioners as well as from pregnant teenagers and young parents and sometimes the responses to our findings and recommendations have included some professional defensiveness. The significant power dimension here is that practitioners and professionals (who are more likely to read the final report, attend the sub-committee or conference where we present our findings and so on) often have more opportunity to challenge the researcher team than the clients/consumers of their 'service', and thus influence the subsequent research outputs, unless a right to respond for all respondents is built into the research.

There is evidence that both providers and clients/consumers of services are likely to welcome research that takes their experience seriously and is likely to improve the services they receive. Jane Royle *et al.* (2001: 10) in their guide for consumers who want to be actively involved in health research quote some research respondents' motivations for involvement. These include:

As 'ordinary people' we get involved in research because we see a possible benefit to ourselves or others we have empathy with.

Being valued, making a meaningful contribution.

To increase the credibility of the service user's voice.

To help people have a voice.

When you are campaigning from personal anecdotes they really don't get listened to, but if you have got a proper programme of research, the knowledge can be used in an objective (*sic*) argument that the authorities have got to live with.

Similarly, many of the respondents in the 'Young Parents' projects have spoken positively about being involved in the research:

It's been good this, good to talk.

(Emma, health professional)

Let them know how we are feeling.

(Shelley, young mother)

We will talk if we get a chance.

(Young fathers' focus group)

They also indicate that they hope that their involvement will lead to a better experience for pregnant teenagers and young parents generally.

As our first project in this area was completed in 2001 and we are still undertaking work with the same provider/client group, we sometimes meet individuals we spoke to several years ago. Rather than annoyance that we want to speak to them again, we have found that respondents value the fact that we are still interested in their stories four/five years later. We suggest that responses of this kind indicate that respondents not only find their involvement in the research valuable in its own right but also have their own political motives for involvement.

Positive relationships with respondents (both providers and clients) are, of course, essential for an extended social research agenda and, therefore, researchers need to think carefully about how to present findings that are critical of current service provision so as not to alienate those individuals who are significant in implementing research findings (see Chapter 7 for more discussion).

Ethics and ethical approval

In addition to detail on proposed method and approach, respondent group, analysis and timescales, research bids need to make reference to issues of ethics. However, although ethics are relevant to the whole of the extending research process, current ethical approval processes relate largely to research during fieldwork; not beyond.

Following the acceptance and funding of a proposal the research team then need to obtain ethical approval, which can be a lengthy process. In brief:

> Ethics are about the moral position adopted by the researcher and those funding that piece of research. Each of these groups has a moral obligation to protect people from any mistreatment which could result from taking part in the research itself.
>
> (Robertson and Dearling 2004: 33)

The benefits of taking ethical issues seriously are obvious and include providing confidentiality for the respondents, taking regard of health and safety issues for the respondents and researchers and ensuring that required codes of practice have been followed. But ethics are not just about individual 'good behaviour' and the discourse on ethics has been influenced by the drive for greater user involvement and protection as well as the development and maintenance of professional integrity in the research process.

The development of local research ethics committees and the guidelines given for their operation (DHSS 1991) and the Research Governance Arrangements (DoH 2001) have placed informed consent and respondent involvement at the centre of the traditional research process. The focus is on protecting the respondents during fieldwork. The development of ethical guidelines came more out of a sense of protection than empowerment. This is echoed in part of the British Sociological Association's *Statement of Ethical Practice* (BSA 2002, revised 2004). It lists the criteria researchers need to take into account when conducting research as:

- professional integrity;
- relations with and responsibilities towards research participants;
- relationships with research participants;
- covert research;

- anonymity, privacy and confidentiality;
- relations with and responsibilities towards sponsors and/or funders;
- clarifying obligations, roles and rights;
- pre-empting outcomes and negotiations about research;
- obligations to sponsors and/or funders during the research process.

However, adhering to ethical concerns is often more complicated than it first appears – both in relation to the remit and timescale of the traditionally defined research process and in relation to extending social research. By way of an example, we find work by Rose Wiles *et al.* (2005: 3) on informed consent useful. Thus:

> It is also difficult to assess whether consent is 'really' informed. Dilemmas include: the value of signed consent forms; how to assess the ability (or 'competence') of individuals to give informed consent, especially for groups characterized as 'vulnerable'; how to recognise that people want to withdraw from their involvement in a research study; how to avoid gate-keepers denying consent for people to participate or including people who have not truly consented; and whether consent should be restricted to data collection or include the ways that data are interpreted and presented.

Issue	On the one hand . . .	On the other . . .
Should signed consent forms be used?	Ensures that participants know their rights; protects the researcher from later accusations from study participants.	May discourage people from participating. Signed consent is meaningless for some groups. In some areas of research, signed consent may make participants and researchers vulnerable to investigation and prosecution.
Should consent be obtained from parents/guardians/care workers in the case of 'vulnerable' participants, and assent from participants?	The law is unclear. To protect researchers from legal proceedings, consent would be obtained from parents/guardians/care workers as well as participants.	This approach denies people's agency. The onus is on researchers to identify ways to gain informed consent from participants and to allow participation even if other parties dispute this.

Who should data belong to? Should participants give consent to the ways that data are interpreted and used?	Research participants should be able to consent to how 'their' data are to be used (including the use of pseudonyms) and stored.	This limits the freedom of the researcher and curtails the critical nature of the discipline.

In addition, even with reference to fieldwork, let alone beyond, there is evidence to suggest that ethics committees are not the guardians of research ethics that they hope to be. Thus, as Carole Truman writes (2003: 3.25, drawing on Rossiter and colleagues 2000):

A condition of ethical approval being granted, is that LREC ask to be informed of any changes to the research protocol . . . Research methodology is often required to change once research participants become part of the research process, yet the relationship of LRECs to research processes means that some researchers may be reluctant to re-enter the ethical approval process once initial approval has been withdrawn; secondly, the bureaucratic nature of LRECs means that they are not able to respond in a timely or constructive way to genuine ethical concerns which unfold during the course of a study. For this to happen, there needs to be 'a shift in our common-sense understanding of ethics as a property of individuals who monadically reflect on dilemmas . . . it requires a much broader set of activities than is associated with conventional professional ethics' (Rossiter *et al.* 2000: 97).

In addition, any research project is likely to involve satisfying the requirements of several ethical stakeholders. For example, in our 'Young Parents' research we always need to obtain ethical approval from the in-house Coventry University Ethics Committee; we sometimes need to complete an online LREC application, which we then have to defend at one of the monthly meetings of LREC; we sometimes also need to defend our work as ethically adequate to the management committee of an organization within which we hope to collect data (an example being the British Pregnancy Advisory Service in a recent project on young people's experience of termination and miscarriage); and our research practice is guided at all times by the British Sociological Association's ethical guidelines (see above). Sometimes the advice/conditions that researchers must respond to may be contradictory; often they are limited in terms of offering support to researchers working within an extended research agenda.

Serious attention to ethical issues throughout the extending research process poses potential issues and challenges for researchers both methodologically and personally. On a methodological level the research methods may have to be altered to meet ethical considerations and on interpersonal levels the research team has to ensure they maintain good working relations, not only within the team but with the research respondents, funders/commissioners. This raises issues of power relations within the research process, which we explore further in Chapter 6. Given the move to collaborative approaches to research, especially research that is action-orientated, these dilemmas have to be continually revisited throughout the extended research process. Therefore, the consideration of ethics is not just a one-off consideration of ensuring integrity in the process, avoiding mistreatment and setting the framework for good working relations but integral throughout the whole of the extended research process – an issue (as noted above) not currently recognized by ethics committees.

Establishing research teams

The relationships amongst research teams and between the research team and the funder/commissioner are also relevant to the potential for extending social research as good working relationships make it much easier to define common goals and working practices throughout the research process. In addition, an established working relationship between a funder and a research team over a series of projects has implications for extending social research as the recommendations from one project can lead to further research, policy change and evaluation.

In many cases research is carried out by a team of researchers rather than an individual researcher, hence consideration needs to be given to the size and composition and dynamics of the research team. In the setting up of research teams Luis Sanz-Menendez *et al.* (2001) identify the growing trend for 'multi-disciplinary' teams and 'interdisciplinary' work. They regard interdisciplinary work as a fluid dynamic that can affect the behaviour of the researchers. It may be that the funders or commissioners have an expectation of the specialisms that would be brought to the research process, possibly influencing decisions about who should be included in the research team. This might also extend to the way the commissioners feel they can effectively interact with the research team – during the data collection, analysis and output and outcome stages of the research. These interpersonal issues are more than simply whether the team has the expertise to deliver the results. Though their research focuses on interdisciplinary working in the field of bio-sciences, Sanz-Menendez *et al.*'s (2001) work has relevance to social science research. The vast majority of researchers develop their research skills as part of a research team but very few researchers are trained in interdisciplinary working. Having to work in this way can put a strain on the research process and can have implications for the extending research agenda if different members of, or groups within, the team bring different personal, academic and political motivations to the research.

In addition to or instead of requiring interdisciplinarity, some commissioners may require researchers who have a personal connection to the issue that they are researching as they see this as providing added authenticity or bringing greater awareness to the issue. Others may see this as an irrelevance. Some commissioners may feel this would help respondents to open up and provide a level of information that might not be given to researchers who appear to have no connection with the research topic. On the other hand, too close an association may lead to accusations of bias and the inappropriate use of research methods (Wilkinson and Kitzinger 1996).

Overall, the (perceived) skills and abilities of the team members and their 'track record' in terms of research outputs and outcomes can be as much a determining factor of funding as the chosen method and approach in both commissioned and tendered research. In tendering for our initial 'Young Parent' project the previous research interests of the principal investigator (which included research in the areas of parenthood and health) were thought to be useful by the commissioners and in subsequent projects the experience and increasing expertise of the research team was clearly valued.

Any discussion of research teams also needs to make reference to issues of power. Liz Kelly et al. (1994) suggest that it is ironic that so much discussion is given in research accounts to the empowerment of respondents, while the possibility that members of the research community may be experiencing oppression is ignored. Low pay, insufficient information about the project to engage fully with the issues, short contracts that concentrate on the collection of data and not the analysis and writing stages of the project characterize the contract researchers' job. This means that even if there is a possibility for further work beyond the traditional research project the more junior members of a research team are less likely to have the opportunity to be involved in this, which is detrimental to the project as well as the work experience of those involved. Thinking about these issues at the beginning of a project, or even before a project starts, at the bid-writing stage, also has a financial advantage in that costing in a researcher's time at this stage is easier than negotiating for extra money once the project has reached its traditional end. An additional advantage of an established working relationship with a commissioner is that it can provide the opportunity to secure researchers' posts for a longer period of time. One disadvantage of the need to attract money from external sources is the pressure to write the next bid or secure the next contract, which can distract the research team from the output and outcome aspects of a project (see Chapters 7 and 8).

Research teams often include individuals other than those employed by a university. For example, in several of our 'Young Parents' projects, young parents themselves have been involved in data collection and development work (see Chapter 8 for further discussion). This kind of involvement of the respondent group within the extending social research process requires a set of skills and resources not often mentioned in research texts. The issue of whether or not to involve service users or members of the respondent group as fieldworkers is one to be negotiated with commissioners/funders in advance and of course can be a significant lever in terms of what happens to findings as these groups are much less likely than commissioners to accept nothing being done following the research report. Some funding bids require evidence of established partnerships with professionals and/or service users and other stakeholders in the research process. This means that when projects are not funded researchers have to respond to the disappointment of their partners.

Intellectual property rights

The intellectual property rights of research is again an issue that needs to be considered at the beginning rather than the end of the traditional research process. Intellectual property (IP) allows people to own their creativity and innovation in order to control and be rewarded for its use. For the academic this is likely to include the publication of research findings in respected academic outputs. Generally, copyright enables creators (authors) of material to control the way in which that material is used, such as the making and issuing of copies, the use of material in public and its use online. For the creator, copyright also affords rights in relation to distortion and mutilation of such material.

However, as a form of property, the rights to the work can be bought, sold or transferred, wholly or in part, as with any other property. Most commonly in such instances, a commissioning contract will have been agreed that states explicitly who holds the copyright. This may have been set out before the commencement of the work, and must be signed by the creators if they are not ultimately to own the work. In many respects this might be the most satisfactory process, since it may well avoid future complications in terms of ownership and publication (Grinyer 1999). In cases where there is no commissioning contract, the commissioner can still use the work without the permission of the owner for specific purposes where it can be shown that an actual or an implied licence exists. A licence should explicitly state the uses of copyright that it covers. An implied licence may apply where it is clear that work was commissioned to be used for a particular purpose. Researchers who are not subject to a commissioning contract may presume a right of ownership on behalf of the commissioner. However, in these less formal relationships, there appears to be greater freedom in regard to the researcher's use of the material. Whilst permission had to be sought to use the data from our 'Young Parents' projects, commissioners appeared to raise few barriers to its use in academia or the media. In some cases they may not even request sight of such releases of information.

Some of the exceptions to copyright are known by the expression 'fair dealing' and the test applied by the court is based on the economic impact for the owner of the copyright. This exception does not cover the use of large amounts of material and/or making multiple copies, and the use of excerpts should generally include an acknowledgement. Thus, should a commissioning contract have passed ownership to a funder, it may still be possible for the creator to use elements of this work, so long as it is not specifically excluded by the contract. Should researchers maintain the right to use research for academic purposes, despite the intellectual property rights having passed to the commissioning body at the start of the project?

An area that can cause tension between the commissioning body and the researcher is when the former is unhappy with the results of the research undertaken. This could be due to unfavourable findings or the report style not suiting the funder's needs. This may be particularly relevant when the research is undertaken in the policy field, and the 'social scientist's concern to retain a critical and independent stance' comes into conflict with the funder's view of research (Bulmer 1987: 198). Building on Maurice Punch's unrealistic assertion that academic researchers should never sign away their right to publish, Grinyer (1999) also considers the implications of a funder's rejection of a researcher's findings: in particular, whether the researcher should publish the results independently. When copyright has been assigned to the funding body, or there is an implied licence to the same effect, the answer here is undoubtedly 'no', since such a move will not only strain relations between the two parties, but it might also result in litigation. This necessitates the need for continued negotiation between commissioner and researcher (Grinyer 1999). The role of the respondent in the research can become an influencing factor. The researcher and respondents in the research may hold a common view of the results which may differ significantly to the commissioning agent. Could the use of a social justice standpoint be used to challenge the implied licence and potential litigation? This situation is similar to that of whistleblowers: they may in law be defended by the argument that their actions are 'in the public interest' but at the same time may be guilty of breaking a contractual duty to respect confidentiality of their employer. In the case of some government research, researchers are required to sign the Official Secrets Act.

In reality commissioners have a variety of ways of suppressing unwelcome findings. First, they may simply delay the production of a final report by extensive and slow processes of internal consultation on a draft. This happened when a local authority kept under review for several months a research report the CSJ had produced evaluating aspects of their child care services that had been contracted out to a voluntary organization. Second, negotiations about changes of wording or conclusions may reach impasse. Alternatively, third, a report may be accepted but not circulated or published but not publicized. The most celebrated example of this was the Black Report on *Inequalities in Health*

(DHSS 1980), published over an August Bank Holiday but subsequently widely circulated and independently published by public and professional demand. Even if a report is accepted and reaches appropriate decision makers, there is no guarantee that conclusions will be acted on. In our experience, the greater the clarity at the point of the contract, including understanding what the commissioner's interests are and how they may conflict with findings, and the closer the relationship during the research process, the less likelihood that research findings will be suppressed through these or other mechanisms.

Where the positions of the commissioning agent and research team are complementary there will be agreement as to what findings are regarded as 'significant' and how to publicize them and develop an action plan. The converse occurs where there is lack of consensus. Our own experience of the management of intellectual property within the 'Young Parents' projects has been a positive one and one that has been renegotiated throughout the process rather than completely determined in the initial stages of the projects. In this instance the publication of the research – in both academic and media formats – has been mutually beneficial for the research team and for the commissioner. It is when publication of research findings and experiences is not such a happy affair for all parties concerned that problems are likely to occur.

Developing relationships: impact and further research

Although we consider in more detail later developing research relationships (Chapter 6), research outputs (Chapter 7) and research outcomes (Chapter 8), it is relevant here to devote some attention to the reporting stage of our first 'Young Parents' project. We do this to highlight the specific relationship between this project and our extending social research agenda in the young parent research area and to demonstrate more generally the possibility of extending social research across a series of related projects. We begin by detailing our recommendations at the end of the project and the TPPB response to them as this shows the relationship between this project and later projects undertaken in the area of young parenthood:

Supported Semi-Independent Housing for Under 18 Lone Parents: Needs Assessment (Letherby *et al.* 2001)

Policy recommendations

In general

Recommendation: Further research from an 'insider' perspective would make it possible to build on and develop the themes and issues identified here.

Response: Since 2001 we have undertaken several more research projects for Coventry TPPB on the experience of young parenthood. One of the issues that became clear in the 2001 housing project was that pregnant teenagers and young parents were not accessing the services that they were entitled to; particularly maternity services. In response to this Coventry TPPB with Walsall TPPB commissioned a project entitled 'Pregnancy and Post-Natal Experience of Young Women Who Become Pregnant under the Age of 20 Years' which took place in 2002. In addition Coventry TPPB recommended our work to Warwickshire TPPB and Sandwell TPPB and we have since undertaken work for them.

A list of completed and ongoing research and developmental work in this area is listed in Table 5.1.

TABLE 5.1: 'Young Parents' research work undertaken by the Centre for Social Justice

Research

Supported Semi-Independent Housing for Under 18 Lone Parents: Needs Assessment (Letherby *et al.* 2001)

Pregnancy and Post-Natal Experience of Young Women who Become Pregnant under the Age of 20 Years (Letherby *et al.* 2002)

Housing Needs of Young Parents in Warwickshire (Letherby *et al.* 2003)

Experience and Support Needs of 'Young' Fathers in Warwickshire (Letherby *et al.* 2004)

An Evaluation of Specialist Services for Pregnant Teenagers and Young Parents (Brown *et al.* 2005)

Power and Control in the Intimate and Personal Relationships of Pregnant Teenagers and Young Mothers (Brown *et al.* 2006)

Support Prior to and Following Termination and Miscarriage for Young Women (Brady *et al.* 2006)

Discourses of Prevention and Support in Relation to Teenage Pregnancy and Young Motherhood (Wilson ongoing PhD research)

Development work

Development of a Multi-Professional Training Pack – Pregnant Teenagers and Young Parents: Health and Well-Being in Pregnancy, During Birth and Post-Natally (Letherby *et al.* 2003–06, not published)

Training Young Parents to Become Peer Researchers – Lifelong Learning for 'Young Parents' Project (reported in Reid *et al.* 2005)

Development of an Entry and Exit Questionnaire/Interview for Young Parents Who Access Any Form of Supported Housing (reported in Brady *et al.* 2005)

Life Story Boards for Young Parents (Brady 2005–06, not published)

Training for Professionals Supporting Young People in Leicester (Brady and Brown 2006, not published)

Recommendation: Formal support is invaluable but needs to be offered in a non-patronising way – young mothers feel that they are for ever 'being told what to do' and/or 'counselled' and resist this kind of help.

Response: Coventry TPPB encouraged the setting up of – and now supports – a Young Parents' Forum for young people to have their say. (See also the reference to the Training Pack below and Chapter 8 for more detail.)

Recommendation: With the above recommendation in mind, Health and Social Care Professionals need training.

Response: Following the completion of the pregnancy and post-natal experience project (2002) (in which we reiterated the need for training) Coventry TPPB commissioned us to develop a training pack for health and social care professionals who work with pregnant teenagers and young parents. This project is currently being rolled out within the local area (see Chapter 8 for more detail).

With particular reference to housing

Recommendation: Housing support needs to be available for young mothers under 16 who do not have the support of their families or whose families are unable to cope – young women in this age group do not want to go into care.

Recommendation: Support needs to be ongoing – young mothers need practical support and advice about education and work, benefits and housing (including support and advice about moving on from semi-supported accommodation) and emotional support and advice (particularly when they do not have the support of their families/partners). Women in semi-supported housing may need 'extra' support to counter the stigma they may feel when they are easily identifiable.

Recommendation: Care needs to be taken when choosing sites for semi-supported housing to minimize the harassment that young mothers have to face.

Recommendation: Semi-supported housing needs to be just that – practical support including the provision of adequate accommodation and services, some provision of childcare and support to achieve independence. Emotional support is also needed.

Response: One of the reasons for the research being commissioned at the time was that it was intended to build a new semi-supported housing complex in the city. Coventry TPPB ensured that the architect of this building used our research report as a blueprint. A real concern for the young parents in the existing semi-supported housing in Coventry was lack of privacy. Because the only doors to individual living space were off a central, communal lounge young women felt that their comings and goings and those of any visitors they had were open to scrutiny. Following the research the new building still has a communal space but each personal living space has its own front door.

Although the site for the new building was already determined there has subsequently been a considerable effort to build positive relationships with the local community. In addition, following the research a sub-group of the TPPB focusing specifically on housing need was established. Various housing providers sit on this committee as well as the Teenage Pregnancy Coordinator for support and researchers from the CSJ. The original brief of this committee related to the recommendations above and the agenda has developed in line with new concerns. Further development work has since been undertaken in relation to semi-supported housing this time including the new and established provision (see Chapter 8).

It may appear from the above, and from this chapter generally, that we encountered few problems in our relationship with the commissioners of our 'Young Parents' projects and it is fair to say that overwhelmingly this experience of research has been a positive one – both for us as researchers and for the TPPB. However, this does not mean that the work has been without challenge. For example, the negative discourses surrounding teenage pregnancy have sometimes resulted in our commissioners and ourselves having to defend our work in this area; at times we have found access to particular respondent groups difficult; and challenging the practice of practitioners and professionals whom we have got to know quite well throughout the research is a downside of working so closely with commissioners and stakeholders.

In terms of extending the research boundaries beyond the traditional limits, we have already noted the continued involvement with practitioners and with policy development to which this initial project has led. But this has resulted in further (initially unexpected) problems. When we began the project we did not envisage the impact it would have, not least on us as researchers. Having spent more than five years researching and writing up the experience of individuals (particularly women) who experience infertility and involuntary childlessness, Gayle (the grant applicant and principal investigator in many of the 'Young Parent' projects) hoped that the work that she did would have some influence on the actual experience of the people she researched and others like them. Nearly ten years on she has written several pieces connected to this research, which several people (mostly other academics) have read, and her work in this area has helped her in terms of promotion and standing in her discipline. Yet, the impact on 'real world' experience is insignificant. In contrast, five years after the first, three-month long, project on young parenthood, several more projects and more importantly a significant number of policy initiatives have followed. Members of the original research team are sitting on each of the two sub-committees of the Coventry TPPB (another was established following the pregnancy and postnatal project to champion the resultant findings and recommendations) and on the TPPB itself. We have also representing the TPPB at regional and national meetings and events and our work in this area has led to the need to develop new skills, including producing and delivering training for practitioners and training young parents to undertake research and be involved in development work.

We will return to these issues in following chapters. The point we wish to make here is that the substantial resources these continuing involvements take – both in terms of time and effort – were not part of our original research costing and, indeed, do not form a direct part of any research contract. This has meant that we have had to and continue to 'play catch up' in terms of some of the more traditionally accepted academic outputs for our projects in this area (see Chapter 7). This is why we are now arguing for the full costs of such an extended research agenda to be included at the bid/proposal stage in order to resource the time and effort of the research team. However, we know that the voluntary work that we have done and continue to do for the TPPBs with whom we have connections has led to more paid work for us. Also, if one's commitment to an extended research agenda is political as well as academic then there is a debate to be had about the ethics of costing. This may sound naïve in the current academic climate of public accountability but it is further demonstration of research experience as less than 'hygienic'.

In some ways, then, our work in the young parent area has had a negative impact on the 'CV building' of the researchers involved and has been not so good for their academic careers. Yet, the extra personal and political pleasure this extended involvement has brought the researchers, and the opportunity it has afforded us to develop 'extra-academic' skills – both in terms of interpersonal relationships and the production of development work material – are important in terms of our extended research approach. Perhaps the problem here then is that, as yet, this approach receives less academic credit than it should?

End points

In this chapter we have begun our consideration of the extending research process through a focus on the initial stages of the process. As such we have begun our challenge of the traditional view of the research process and highlighted the need to reflect on potential opportunities and problems in terms of research outcomes and outputs at the point of or even prior to starting the research. Towards the end of the chapter we turned our attention to developing research relationships and in Chapter 6 we continue our challenge to the traditional model through further attention to managing the process of research.

Notes

1. The researched are variously referred to as respondents, subjects, participants or informants. 'Subjects' (which can imply full involvement but is also reminiscent of people having things done to them and of people who belong to others) and 'informants' (people from whom others get information) are often avoided in research writings. Some researchers, with the aim of equalizing the researcher/respondent relationship, have begun to use the term 'participants'. But this is problematic also, as it implies an equality in the research process that is rarely achievable. With this in mind we use the term respondents when referring to individuals in our research projects (see also Letherby 2003a).

6

Managing the process

Anthea Coghlan, Gayle Letherby, Denise Tanner,
Corinne Wilson and Paul Bywaters

*Introduction • Steering groups • Building and maintaining relationships
• Analysis • Commissioner responses • End points*

Introduction

Recently, the view that within social research the roles of respondent, researcher and commissioner are discrete has been challenged, not least by the growth of user-focused and user-controlled research. Although researchers are likely to have more power at various points in the research process, it is not the case that the researcher is all-powerful and the respondent completely powerless (e.g. Maynard and Purvis 1994; Hood et al 1999; Letherby 2003a). However, in developing an extending social research approach it is necessary to think again about power within the research process, for involvement throughout the process is essential to involvement beyond the boundaries of traditional research endings. With this in mind we explore in this chapter the ethical perspectives and the knowledge and skills necessary for the engagement of all interested parties or stakeholders throughout the research process and the relevance of this to extending social research. We do not, however, argue for full engagement in every case but for a reflexive position that *always* considers the significance of stakeholder involvement in the research process.

There is clearly a whole range of levels of possible and potential stakeholder involvement. Respondents, research commissioners and other individuals who may be affected by the research outcomes may be members of a steering group or co-researchers. Researchers may be 'service users' and share key social and economic characteristics and experiences of inequality and oppressive social relations with research respondents, perhaps differing in terms of their specific role within the research but sharing other significant aspects of identity. Commissioners may influence the research process, and the involvement of themselves and respondents in and beyond the research, through enabling or restricting access to respondents or by restricting the publication and presentation of findings.

In Chapter 5, we began to consider the implications of adopting an extended approach to research by focusing on the beginnings of the process. Following on from this, we now consider further the significance of extending social research across the research process. Here we are primarily concerned with the data collection and analysis elements of the research process and how the processes through which these are carried out influence the eventual outputs and outcomes of research. We do not, of course, cover everything that could be said about extending social research in managing the process of research but provide some illustrative examples. These cover, first, a focus on the formation and operation of steering groups and second, building and maintaining relationships during the research process. Towards the end of the chapter we discuss respondent involvement in and commissioner response to data analysis. Here, as in Chapter 5, we draw on commissioned work undertaken by researchers from the Centre for Social Justice (CSJ) especially the 'Young Parents' projects; a project concerned with institutional racism within the regional branch of a national charity and another which focused on older people refused a service by social services.

With reference to our key principles, of specific relevance here is the assertion that the primary purpose of social research is to change the human condition (principle 1); plus our views that extending social research has implications for the whole process – all stages are extended (principle 4); if researchers take responsibility for what happens to their findings, they need to learn new skills – researchers' roles are extended (principle 5); and if this approach is adopted by researchers, it has implications for funders, partners, expected beneficiaries and end users of research – research relationships are extended (principle 6) (see Chapter 1, p. 5, Table 1.1).

Steering groups

Alister Scott and colleagues (1999) argue for the need for continuous discussion and interaction between researchers and commissioners, through which the research agenda is jointly set and there is agreement about flexibility within the research process. Sometimes these issues are addressed when discussing intellectual property rights (see Chapter 5), but often they are assumed to be the core remit of the research steering group. In other words, steering groups can play a central part in setting up effective research. They can act as advisers, as sounding boards, as providers of local and other knowledge, as representatives of interest groups, as resources for respondents, as critics of interim reports and ongoing data analysis, and as allies in the extension of the work of the project beyond traditional boundaries.

There are very varied ways in which Steering Groups can be set up. Funders or commissioners may identify members, with the researcher(s) having little or no involvement in the process, or researchers may work with the funders or commissioners to identify appropriate people to be in the group. As well as careful consideration of individual membership, attention also needs to be given to the balance between representative parties; for example, service users may play an active role in determining who is to be on the steering group, and seek a balance between professional input and service user input. In some cases it can prove difficult to involve individuals or groups in steering groups for a variety of reasons – lack of interest, lack of time, lack of resources – and this can have implications for the research process within and beyond traditional boundaries. In addition, other factors may prevent a group being representative of all stakeholders, whatever the intentions. Some of the work of the Centre for Social Justice (CSJ) has been around refugees and asylum seekers where respondents may fear identification by the authorities, may be moved on, or 'dispersed' at any moment and, therefore, there is no possibility of a semi-permanent group who can provide 'representatives' to participate in a steering group.

There are of course potential tensions to consider. Bringing people together from across an 'organizational' spectrum can be both a potentially fruitful and disastrous strategy. Fruitful, in that it can enable people to contribute different perspectives and provide a transparent forum for the management of the process where agendas can be brought out in the open, where the researcher can be seen as an 'honest broker'. Disastrous, if people exercise differential power negatively within the group, confidentiality is not respected, there are differing degrees of commitment and ownership of the process and the researcher is regarded as being biased towards one perspective. The steering group may fail to agree the research process, or not find common ground on theoretical, conceptual, ethical or practical issues. Steering groups may be given, or take upon themselves, the power to dramatically change the nature, function and remit of the research (which of course has ethical implications, not least in relation to external ethical approval, see Chapter 5). Within this, the role of the researcher may be regulated to that of group secretary or bystander. The group may be subject to a number of power plays being acted out within the group itself, which may prevent it from acting effectively. Here the researcher may have to extend his or her own role and seek to manage the group and the tensions in order to keep the research 'on track'.

In relation to the various 'Young Parent' projects first introduced in Chapter 5, steering groups, which always included stakeholders from key professional groups and in later projects also included young parents, have helped with finding respondents for the research – both young people and professionals – and identifying how best to access them. In many cases the group has also impacted on the whole process of the research; from the generation of research questions and new ideas to the discussion of both interim and (draft) final reports. In some of the later projects, young parents who had been involved in earlier projects or were part of the current one became part of the group and here the researchers, practitioners and young parents worked to their respective strengths and collective goals both in terms of the data collection and the research outputs and outcomes. For example, in both the 'Research on Lifelong Learning for Pregnant Young Women and Young Parents in Sandwell project (Reid *et al.* 2005) and the 'Evaluation of Specialist Services for Pregnant Teenagers and Young Parents' (Brown *et al.* 2005) the young mothers on the steering groups helped to determine the parameters of the project and develop the qualitative interview schedule, and were involved in data collection and commented on/contributed to analysis.

Our experience has not always been so positive though. The CSJ was asked by the regional management team of a national charity which provided a range of services, primarily through local projects, to review whether and how services in the region might have been 'institutionally racist' and to make recommendations for ways of 'dealing with the issue'. In this context, institutional racism was seen as any other discrete part of an organizational issue – as having defined boundaries and clearly observable aspects that could be scrutinized and repaired. In the 'Institutional Racism' project staff input was gained through the use of a questionnaire and focus group interviews and service users' views were canvassed through focus group interviews alone. The project was supported by a steering group composed of the regional director, two assistant directors and two project managers from the commissioning agency and all three members of the research team. In terms of composition there were three white males, three white females (including two of the researchers) and two black males (a researcher and the chair of the region's black workers' group, which gave the research team access to the national race group within the organization). At first the group appeared to work well together and early meetings were spent discussing common goals and methods and developing the questionnaire to which all steering group members contributed. The steering group facilitated the distribution of this jointly produced questionnaire across the organization and we waited expectantly for the data to roll in.

Given Tim May's (1997: 90–1) assertion that '. . . unless people have an incentive, either through an interest in the subject . . . or some other basis, then response rates are likely to be low and the figure of 40 per cent is not uncommon' we were disappointed that our initial response rate was 14.5 per cent. In response to this, some of the organizational members of the steering group said that they thought that the questionnaire, which immediately became *yours* (the research team's) rather than *ours* (the steering group's), was 'too academic'. However, from the research findings (which we refer to again later in the chapter), it also appears that some potential respondents may have been anxious that they might appear uninformed concerning racist issues and this might be seen to reflect on their practice. This is likely to have contributed to the low response rate.

Having received the initial 25 responses, members of the steering group encouraged their colleagues to return the questionnaires and to fill them in 'in the best ways that they could', ignoring questions that they felt were unclear and commenting on the things that they felt were wrong with the questionnaire. Following this we had another 22 responses (27 per cent response rate overall), all of which were fully completed. We received no substantial written criticisms of the questionnaire. From then on the relationship between the research team and the organizational members of the steering group was tense. This impacted on the rest of the data collection process, the reception given to the research findings and the subsequent impact of the research – again we return to this later in the chapter.

Anne Grinyer (1999), drawing on a model suggested by Scott *et al.* (1999), argues that there should be continuous discussion and interaction between researchers and commissioners, during which agendas are jointly set and there is agreement regarding developments and changes of direction. In hindsight, an early discussion within a steering group meeting about how to deal with negative responses to the research may have prevented the breakdown in positive relations later. However, other agendas within an organization may also affect attitudes towards involvement in research. In this case, recent restructuring within the organization had left a legacy of uncertainly and insecurity.

Building and maintaining relationships

Access

Who researchers do and do not access as respondents within a research project has implications specifically for building and maintaining relationships within and beyond the field and generally for the research process and product and for possible outputs and outcomes. With this in mind it is important that research reports include reference to any limitations with/omissions from the respondent group so that this can be taken into account during the planning of outcomes. In all of the 'Young Parent' projects so far, the majority of young people respondents have been white. Thus, it is important to note that the young women we have spoken to have not reflected the diversity of the West Midlands in terms of ethnicity. As Lynn Weber Cannon *et al.* (1991) note, researchers who are committed to incorporating respondents from diverse ethnic groups in their work must be prepared to allow more time and money for respondent recruitment and data collection. For example, to access some minority communities it may be necessary to produce research requests in several different languages or to put time into building relationships. However, as most of the respondents in our research were recruited via the support services that they access, the lack of diversity in our respondent group is likely to reflect the fact that the services themselves are predominantly accessed by white women. This raises several important questions. Are services meeting the needs of ethnic minorities? Do ethnic minority groups know about the services available? Are the experiences of this group different? In other words, do issues around 'race' and racism provide an additional dimension to the experience of these groups? Is there still an assumption that ethnic minorities 'look after their own'? Are the services located in areas where all groups have easy access?

With reference to issues of class and income groupings, although we did access young women respondents across a range of income groups the majority of the young women were from lower income groupings. Arguably, this reflects the fact that, in the West Midlands of the UK at least, 'Local data indicates that there is a relationship between under-18 conception rates and deprivation with the highest areas of deprivation correlating with the highest areas of teenage conception (Coventry TPPB 2002). However, this data does not include private termination figures and young women from higher income groups may very well be accessing these services. Access to young people respondents under the age of 16 was also problematic in that parental consent in additional to respondent consent is needed for this group. The fact that proportionately we spoke to fewer under-16s than over-16s likely reflects the differences in terms of surveillance, control and stigma (Letherby *et al.* 2002; Brown et al. 2006) for this group.

Methods and methodological experience

Many researchers suggest that qualitative methods enable respondents to influence the direction of the research and encourage participatory researcher/ respondent relationships (Oakley 1981; Reinharz 1983) within and beyond the traditional boundaries of the research process. As noted in Chapter 5, qualitative research methods also enable researchers to explore issues of concern to themselves and to respondents in greater depth than would be possible with larger groups. With this in mind, following the initial analysis of the 'Institutional Racism' questionnaire, the researchers prepared for a number of focus groups: one with the Black Workers' Group; two with project workers; one with representatives from Head Office and two with service users. However, although the research team asked for individuals to volunteer for focus group participation via a tear-off slip on the questionnaire, only four individuals volunteered. Even when the research team wrote directly to project staff and service users about the purpose, value and structure and ethical dimensions of this aspect of the data collection only a few more members of the organization volunteered for the focus groups. In the end, the following groups took place: one with the Black Workers' Group (two people); one with project workers (three people, although we were expecting a larger number to turn up); two with service users (15 people). Given the small numbers, the research team decided not to undertake a focus group with representatives from Head Office so as not to 'skew' the data in favour of the 'management perspective'.

As other researchers have noted, providing space to talk about taboo topics may bring forward vulnerable people who have little opportunity to talk about their experience elsewhere. This may mean that individuals involved in this type of research end up 'giving away' more than they later feel comfortable with (e.g. see Finch 1984; Cotterill and Letherby 1994). On the other hand, a questionnaire is a way for individuals to be involved in research anonymously (not just in the final analysis and presentation of the data but during the data collection) (Kelly *et al.* 1994). In the 'Institutional Racism' project it seems that neither approach was ideal. The fact that it was as difficult to recruit respondents to the focus group stage of the fieldwork as to the questionnaire stage throws doubt on the 'questionnaire being too hard' explanation (even though questionnaires do not allow for further explanation and clarification during data collection). Research does not take place in a vacuum and the sensitivity of the issue under investigation, plus the changes taking place in the organization at that time (see above) are likely to have affected the project.

Although our experience of working on the 'Young Parent' projects has been overwhelmingly positive, the research team has been and remains challenged by various methodological dilemmas. In relation to issues of participation and involvement the research team is uncomfortable with writing that seems to suggest that children are a distinct and therefore difficult group to research (see also Harden *et al.* 2000). As adults researching children we recognize that in some ways we are 'representing the other' (Wilkinson and Kitzinger 1996). However, our experience leads us to suggest that children and young people are less 'other' than is often suggested. We, like others, are suggesting here that power within research is not one-dimensional/one-directional but rather is negotiable and moves from and between researcher and respondent (e.g. Cotterill 1992; Collins 1998; Letherby 2003a). However, we appreciate the importance of acknowledging when the researcher does have the balance of power. One dimension of the researchers' power is the power to define, reflected in 'Young Parent' researcher teams' ongoing struggle around research language. Is, for example, young woman a respectful way to address a 14-year-old female parent, or is it denying the legitimate status of girlhood?

Talking about one's own experiences can be a way for researchers to 'give something back' to respondents (e.g. Oakley 1981) and was something that the 'Young Parents' researchers aimed to do in single and focus group interviews. However, it is possible to argue, yet again, that this kind of disclosure by researchers can encourage respondents to say things that they later regret. Some respondents may also have expectations of the researcher and the research that are unrealistic (Cotterill and Letherby 1994). For example, in the 'Supported Semi-Independent Housing for under 18 Lone Parents: Needs Assessment' project (Letherby *et al.* 2001), one respondent, Sandra, said:

Will you be able to sort housing? Will housing be sorted out when you have done these interviews? Can you sort out housing?

Respondents were/are fully informed of the purpose and aims of the project and made aware that their participation is voluntary, both verbally, and by way of a 'Participant Information Sheet'. Respondents are free to withdraw at any time and assured that they do not have to answer any questions that they would rather not. Yet, sometimes involvement 'brings up' issues for respondents, which results in emotional distress. However, as many researchers have argued, it is important not to ignore particular research topics because of the danger of emotion and indeed sometimes emotional expression is data in itself (e.g. Lee-Treweek and Linkogle 2000). Despite the occasional display of distress all of the young people respondents in the 'Young Parent' project have spoken positively about their involvement in the study and indeed many felt very positively about the attention being given to the issue and their role in raising the issues of concern to young parents.

An approach of involving a sub-section of research respondents as co-researchers was taken a stage further in a research project carried out with older women as part of the Economic and Social Research Council (ESRC) 'Growing Older' programme (Cook *et al.* 2003). The project was concerned with exploring factors that shape quality of life for older women from different ethnic backgrounds and it was designed from the beginning as 'change-oriented' research. It adopted a participatory approach in which ten older women were recruited as 'volunteers', from a total of 100 older women who participated in discussion groups. The volunteers were trained to carry out individual interviews with other older people, help analyse the information and participate in promoting and evaluating change. They played a key role in publicizing the project findings and recommendations. The outcomes included a presentation by the volunteers at a major launch event and the production of a video featuring respondents talking about the project and its recommendations about services and involvement. The video has been used with local community groups, service providers, policy makers and in student education to increase understanding of older women's needs and experiences. A guidance document for running discussion groups and influencing practice has also been published as an outcome of the research (Cormie and Warren 2001).

The participatory approach used in this project raised issues concerning research boundaries. Some older women who acted as gatekeepers in the recruitment of other older women were included in the discussion groups but had a tendency to become 'dominant voices' within the groups, particularly where they were also acting as interpreters. Other issues identified from the participatory approach included the tendency for respondent-researchers recruited to work with the research team to be the younger, more active, vocal and English-speaking older women. The need to allow for adequate time and resources in the research design for preparing research respondents for involvement in analysis and presentation was also highlighted. In this study the intrinsic personal benefits emanating from involvement in the research, such as increased self-confidence, were valued by respondents as much as improvements in services.

In the cumulative series of projects concerned with the status and experience of young parents, the views and experiences communicated by young people, and those that support them both formally (professionals and practitioners) and informally (partners, family and friends) in single and focus group interviews, have informed the future process and direction of the project and further projects. As this chapter aims to demonstrate, generating change as a result of research cannot be separated from processes and relationships at other stages of the research. Research respondents are unlikely to be involved in promoting change if they have not had some earlier involvement in the research since commitment to the change agenda will depend, to a significant extent, on their ownership of the recommendations and proposals. However, experience of involvement in research indicates that involvement in earlier parts of the process by no means implies automatic involvement at the stage of drawing conclusions or implementing change. Whilst respondents may be involved in deciding on research questions, planning and overseeing research processes and data gathering, there is generally less attention given in the literature to the involvement of respondents in analysing data, drawing conclusions, making recommendations and implementing action plans (Beresford 2002, 2003).

In contrast to this position the 'Training Young Parents to Become Peer Researchers – Lifelong Learning for Young Parents' project (Reid *et al.* 2005) involved young mothers at all stages of the research. The project began with peer interviewer training which involved several sessions led by a member of the CSJ 'Young Parent' research team, the lead researcher for the project and four young mothers. These preparatory sessions included:

• thinking about issues and stereotypes around teenage pregnancy and young parenthood and around lifelong learning;

- formulating research questions and themes;
- practical dilemmas whilst undertaking interviews;
- emotional dilemmas whilst undertaking interviews;
- issues of power and control during interviews;
- practice interviewing.

Attention was also given to issues of confidentiality both within the interview team and within interviews. A support network between the peer interviewers and the lead researcher was established, which continued throughout the fieldwork. Following the first focus group interviews, which took place at a local 'Teen Parents Speak Out' conference, a further training event took place to discuss fieldwork experience so far and adapt the interview 'aide memoir'. Following the completion of the data collection an additional session focusing on analysis and evaluation took place. The research team, including the peer researchers, then presented the work – in written and verbal presentation format – to the commissioners and at a regional conference aimed at professionals who work with pregnant teenagers and young parents. The 'insider' status of the peer researchers added to the project in that their own experience was a guide to pertinent issues for exploration and data analysis and in terms of their identification with young pregnant women and young parent respondents and vice versa. However, this 'insider' status was problematic in that some of the data highlighted criticism of the services and support that the peer researchers were themselves accessing. When reporting back (midway through the project) at a multi-agency consultation meeting with professionals it looked as though the peer researchers were being critical of the professionals who were working with them and this could have affected their working relationships:

> *Peer researcher*: It's been really hard like when I said before with people looking at [me] [when speaking at the conference] and when I talked about [name of supported housing . . .] and it seemed like it was going to be crap and I think I said it in as many words and they just gasped and then I explained that it wasn't what I thought now and it is nice but I thought 'are you going to listen to me or what?'

On reflection, perhaps this could have been overcome if the research team had had a meeting with the key workers to explain the status of the peer researchers and to separate their identity as researchers from their identity as young parents and 'clients'.

Childcare was also an issue affecting all the peer researchers' participation. For example:

> *Peer researcher*: I told them I can't get anyone to look after Charlie and they said they would get someone so I could do it and they

> sorted it out two or three times and I've done the rest. I
> don't think it is fair as everyone else gets paid for their
> childcare workers but I'm looking after him myself so no
> childcare worker has had to be paid ... if I did it again I
> wouldn't want him there as I can't concentrate and I'd like
> to listen and be 100 per cent focused but I can't.

The length of the project was another issue raised by peer researchers. They felt that the research and the researcher training should have been for longer. If a longer time period had been available we could have run the training and group interviews over a longer period and then held the one-to-one interviews. This would have provided the peer researchers with more experiences and confidence to interview independently.

As noted in Chapter 5, the ongoing positive relationship between the researchers and the research commissioners of the 'Young Parent' projects has been a crucial ingredient in producing change and facilitating young people's involvement in these processes. The continuing nature of the projects and the intersecting roles and relationships of researchers, research commissioners and key professionals has meant that the researchers have an ongoing role in accomplishing the changes proposed by the research. They, in turn, build in as part of the research process the involvement of the young people in achieving these. Basic parameters of the projects in terms of timescales and funding have also been significant factors. Whereas involving the young people in research processes, particularly implementing change, was more difficult in earlier projects when the timescale was very short and contracts with research staff short-term, this has been facilitated by the longer timescales and more permanent staffing characteristic of the later projects.

The examples of research projects considered here encompass various levels and types of respondent involvement in processes of analysis, interpretation and implementing change. There are a number of points that can be highlighted from these various examples.

First, it is crucial to build in from the start of the process the necessary resources, including time, financial support (including money for childcare when appropriate) and training, to support respondent involvement in analysis, reporting and implementing change. It is also necessary to recognize that while respondents may need support to develop particular skills in order to engage in a meaningful way in research processes, the onus for change does not all rest with them. Respondent involvement has a ripple effect, requiring and prompting other sorts of changes, and involving respondents will itself have an impact on research methodologies, methods and processes. For example, consultation with service users about research ethics suggests they have different views about the requirements for ethical research (Beresford 2003). If respondents are to be involved in analysis, publicizing findings and implementing change, research processes themselves have to be rendered comprehensible, accessible and user-friendly. As we shall see in Chapters 7 and 8, projects involving respondents have outputs and outcomes, not just through traditional means of written reports and verbal presentations, but also through more innovative approaches such as the use of video and drama. As well as being methods of presentation preferred by respondents, such mechanisms may have a more potent impact on target audiences.

Second, there is no one right way of 'doing' respondent/user involvement in research and different projects may encompass different levels and types of involvement. There needs to be absolute clarity with respondents from the outset of the research about the possibilities and limitations of their involvement, on the one hand, and their preferences and choices, on the other. Research respondents will have different motivations for becoming involved in research (including, like professional researchers, financial reward) and will want different things from it. Some may want some of the intrinsic personal benefits emanating from the process of involvement without responsibilities that extend beyond the contributing of data. While researchers need to assume responsibility for extending opportunities for, and removing barriers to participation, a range of types and levels of involvement should be available, with each individual's preferences respected.

Third, finding ways to work with respondents on what happens as a consequence of the research is more likely to effect change in line with the values of social justice. Research can be used as a substitute for action, to delay change and retain control in certain hands (Davis 1992). Recent research with black and minority ethnic older people has highlighted their disillusionment with research that asks the same questions and/or produces the same findings. They want not more research but rather action to bring about change (Butt and O'Neil 2004). Involving respondents in all stages of the research process is likely to increase the impetus for change since service user knowledge, based as it is on direct experience, tends to feature a greater concern with action (Beresford 2000). Moreover, it will help to ensure that priorities for change identified from research reflect concerns significant to the people whose lives are most directly affected by the issues in question.

Fourth, in evaluating research outcomes it is important to define this broadly, in ways that include improvements to services, the achievement of greater influence and control for respondents and others likely to be affected by the research findings and possible therapeutic benefits for research respondents. In other words, planning and evaluating change should take account of the consumerist, democratic and therapeutic purposes of participation (Braye 2000). Change comes in many shapes and sizes. While the concern of academic researchers has traditionally been with research outputs in terms of books, journal articles and conference papers, and of professionals with research outcomes such as policy or service changes, research respondents are more likely to measure change in terms of the difference it makes to their daily life or that of other people in similar situations. It is important that we do not operate with fixed and exclusive ideas about what change involves or how it is achieved. The very fact of respondent involvement challenges existing understandings and changes 'the rules of the game' (Ellis and Rummery 2000). The involvement of research participants can add different voices and perspectives to all stages of the research process; this is likely to open up diverse ways of understanding and interpreting 'findings' and different ways of thinking about, accomplishing and evaluating change.

All four issues could be ascribed the tag of 'added value'. The very dimension commissioners and funders of research, especially government departments, are looking for is the very thing that is regarded as an extra cost, though expected under the label of 'service user involvement'. The power of the commissioner or funder cannot be ignored here: the power to determine not only what is researched but often to determine how it is researched. Within this, researchers are constantly seeking new ways to have effective respondent involvement in which the relationship between the researcher and respondent is crucial. This itself can have an impact on the wider issues in terms of the power relations between commissioners and respondents of research.

Analysis

Analysis is often not something that happens just at the end of a project but is, or at least should be, ongoing. This means, then, that change can occur through processes as well as outcomes, and can occur during the research and not only at, or after, its conclusion. A graphic illustration of change occurring during the research process is given by Kathleen Pitcairn (1994), who relates the situation of a female resident of a hostel for people with learning disabilities. When Pitcairn was carrying out research at the hostel, she observed that the woman's abilities were far greater than staff had assumed. When a reassessment of the woman's needs was instigated, it transpired that she had a physical but not a learning impairment, yet she had been labelled, marginalized and subjected to inappropriate intervention on the basis of her assumed learning disability for many years. In terms of research generating change, this illustrates the importance of taking account of changes that occur within research processes, as well as 'end' outcomes, and changes at individual as well as broader social levels. In focusing on how researchers and respondents are involved in the processes of change through research, it is relevant to consider areas such as the development of individual skills and confidence, changing relationships within the research process and changes to the planned process of the research as well as more specific and final outcomes that relate to changes in policies, practices and services. All of these areas are of course intertwined with power relationships amongst and between all of those involved.

In the project on older people refused a service by social services, the researcher – Denise Tanner – offered all her respondents the opportunity to contribute to analysis. However, they did not all wish to participate in this way, having different views about what they wanted from involvement in the study. This ranged from one person who was very interested in all aspects of the study and asked to be sent anything Tanner wrote to someone who only wanted involvement in the interviews. Only five respondents engaged in any substantial discussion about the reports and, of these, three made written comments on the reports. Others were quite clear that they did not like paper-work or writing; while they enjoyed talking to Denise, liked reading about the situations of others or were interested in what changes might happen as a result of the study, they did not see any value in terms of involvement in the wider research processes. In this study, the analysis was shared with respondents during the fieldwork stage (which lasted three years) rather than following final analysis and it is likely that respondents' understanding of the analysis shared with them influenced the content of later interviews. For example, the analysis highlighted respondents' determination and resource-fulness in finding strategies to 'keep going' in the face of difficulties. This may have reinforced the significance of positive social presentations, making it harder for them to acknowledge difficulties in later interviews in case this was seen as failing or 'giving in'.

A critical factor in involving respondents in commenting on research find-ings is the presentation of the written report in a clear, concise and accessible format. Producing a clear, concise account that goes beyond factual details and includes theoretical reflection is a challenge and one that if not adequately addressed can reinforce inequalities of power and possibly alienate respond-ents (Standing 1998). In her research, Tanner checked out style and language with family and friends, including an older person who had received limited education, who could read the report from a 'lay perspective'. Being able to communicate in a clear and direct style is not only important when sharing analysis with respondents but also enables research findings to be published in ways that allow conclusions and possibilities for action or change to be more easily understood and owned (Osborn and Willcocks 1990). The knowledge and skills traditionally required for academic activity and research are different from, and perhaps sometimes antithetical to, those required to engage mean-ingfully with respondents *and* commissioners of research in the actual 'doing' of and presentation of research (Beresford 2000; Braye 2000).

When older people were commenting on the findings of the 'Older People Refused a Service by Social Services' project, it was the 'facts' and detail that appeared to be of interest rather than the 'theorizing'. In the report, the 'find-ings' from the first two interviews were presented according to themes that were illustrated with 'case' examples and quotations. This was followed by 'theorizing' about the significance of identity and then presentation of a num-ber of suggested practice implications for preventive services for older people. Respondents were not particularly keen on talking about the 'theorizing' around identity issues but were generally more interested in making compar-isons between their own situation and that of others highlighted in the report (which contributed to further 'academic' theorizing around the social basis of identity). Respondents also commented on the recommendations about 'what should be done'. This is perhaps not surprising and may reflect their concern with a different type of theorizing rather than a lack of interest in theory *per se* (Gubrium and Wallace 1990), in particular, a greater concern with theory that relates directly to action and change (Beresford 2000).

Seeking comments from respondents on the ongoing analysis of data through the reports had a direct impact on the approach taken to analysis, so this in itself generated change. One respondent was unhappy that her dialogue from the interviews had been dissected into chunks and repeated out of context in the report. This prompted the researcher to consider the limitations of an analytical approach based on fragmenting and decontextualizing interview accounts and the advantages of examining them as integrated narratives. In response to this, the interview transcripts and diary entries were reread and analysed as 'whole narratives', which supplemented and enriched the existing analysis. In addition, in order to present respondents as 'whole persons' in the research report, the researcher also produced, in discussion with respondents, a 'pen picture' of each individual against which quotations could be cross-referenced.

As well as influencing research processes and the sense made of the data gathered, the experiences and views of respondents also had an effect on extending social research at all stages of the process, in that it had a direct impact on local policy and practice during the process of the study. For example, early interviews identified that respondents who had been referred to social services for help with tasks around the home were sent a glossy brochure detailing private sector providers throughout the county. In discussing with respondents whether they had found this useful in finding help, a number of them commented that it was 'useless'. Many of the providers were located elsewhere in the county, the majority of the information concerned residential care providers and those domiciliary care agencies that were listed tended to provide personal care rather than the more general home care assistance needed by respondents. The cost of the brochure, marked on the back page but not charged to respondents, was £5. The respondents who had received this brochure considered it a waste of council resources and also a waste of their time and effort in contacting agencies that then said they only provided personal care. This information was relayed back to social service managers who stopped the practice of sending out the brochure where referrals concerned help with home care. Instead, Age Concern was contacted to devise locally relevant information as part of the council's preventative strategy. During the course of the study, the researcher was able to feed back these developments to respondents who could see that their views and experiences were having a direct impact on local policy and practice.

Commissioner responses

As we have already established, positive working relationships with commissioners/funders of research are crucial to positive researcher involvement in the extending social research project. As we have also already stated, positive relationships are not inevitable. The nature and parameters of both organizational culture and management in the private, public and voluntary sectors may give us a clue to some of the problems of working with commissioners. As Mark Easterby-Smith and colleagues (1993: 6) observe, managers 'hold considerable power, they are accustomed to controlling, influencing and structuring the awareness of others'. As they go on to argue, managers are unlikely to allow researchers access to an organization unless there is an organizational or personal advantage in conducting the research. They have control of access and can establish conditions that place boundaries around the research process. Easterby-Smith *et al.* (1993) go further to suggest that the research question may also be framed according to the expectations of managers with the emphasis relating to possibilities of access rather than theoretical considerations. Equally significantly, they argue, there may be expectations of action leading to practical outcomes. As regards public service provision, Colin Todhunter (2004) explains that there is a climate of consumerism incorporating consultation with users and, as Anthea Coghlan and Dexter du Boulay (2004) suggest, the very nature of new public management determines an organization culture in which there is a greater responsiveness to consumer demand, a search for excellence and measurable outcomes, and in which research and analysis are tools in this process. Therefore, managers in public services, while recognizing the need to elicit the views of staff and consumers, are also motivated to demonstrate that they are performing effectively.

Our experience of the 'Institutional Racism' project resonates with some of these concerns. Despite discussion of our analysis and emerging findings throughout the research process the steering group expressed surprise at the presentation of findings in the final research report. In the report, the research team recorded key issues arising from the analysis of policies and procedures, questionnaires and focus group interviews. These included:

Policies and procedures

There is a failure to meet the needs of ethnic minorities and relatedly, there is a need for action plans for equal opportunities/anti-discriminatory practice;

The Supervision Policy does not provide clear direction on the use of supervision to review anti-oppressive practice;

The information about legislation is out of date.

Questionnaires

The charity is thought to be institutionally racist;

There has been very little useful formal discussion in the projects and the region on institutional racism;

A number of positive positions/policies and procedures adopted by the Charity do not occur in practice;

This research is seen as the most positive step the Charity is taking to deal with institutional racism;

Mandatory training is the most important thing the Charity could do to tackle institutional racism.

Focus groups with staff members

The Charity is institutionally racist and there is evidence of racist practice: evident in interview process, language, 'lip-service' given to 'political correctness', and in individual encounters.

Focus groups with service users

Service users appear to perceive the Charity as a project level service but they had positive perceptions of service provision.

Following this the research team made a number of recommendations for practice to promote cultural change, stressing that any change needed to be perceived as senior management-driven.

The final steering group meeting where the final report was presented was an uncomfortable experience for all involved. The senior management team members of the steering group appeared to perceive the research findings as a personal critique of their own management practices and criticized the research team once more for their methods and for not providing an easy 'solution' to their problem – something they said they were expecting the research to deliver. This marked the end of the CSJ's relationship with this charity and the end of our involvement in the outcomes of this piece of research. We know there have been several changes at senior management level subsequently but remain unaware of any changes within the organization resulting from our research. Given the limited response following both Lord Scarman's (1981) and Sir William MacPherson's (1993) reports on institutional racism, we remain unsurprised although disappointed about our inability to remain involved in this development work. This outcome reflects the scepticism expressed, during the data collection process, by some black staff that the research would lead to positive change and likely left them feeling that they were more alienated from the organization by the end of the process than they had been at the start. The references to the 'Institutional

Racism' project in this chapter are of course written from our perspective and the organization that commissioned the research very likely has a different view on our relationship and research.

End points

In this, the second chapter concerned with the process of research, we have presented some examples of managing the process of research with an extending social research agenda in mind. The key issue here is that the development of positive relationships with all research stakeholders is valuable not just for the collection of research data but specifically for extending social research. Having considered both the beginning stages and the data and analysis stages of the research process we progress in the next two chapters to the issues of output and outcome.

7

Outputs

Tony Colombo, Paul Allender, Paul Bywaters and Gayle Letherby

Introduction • Research outputs: what works? • Output strategy and audiences • Forms of output • End points

Introduction

Several of our core principles for extending social research are directly relevant to the production of outputs, which we deal with in this chapter, and influencing outcomes, which is the subject of Chapter 8. In contrast to the stance taken in many recent research texts (for example, Blaxter *et al.* 2001; Ritchie and Lewis 2003; Henn *et al.* 2005), we see the production of outputs and outcomes as much more than 'writing up' for primarily academic or research audiences (principle 2). We prefer the term 'reporting' to 'writing up' as it conveys a process of looking outwards and something of the ethical obligation that we have argued that researchers have to share the knowledge they have gained. But even that term seems to imply a one-way process rather than a continuation of the 'sustained interaction' between researcher and research users to which we referred in Chapter 4. As we have argued, and will explore particularly in the following chapter, we see researchers as having an active role to play in applying and implementing research findings, in creating outcomes, in bringing about change, as well as in publicizing them to a variety of audiences. We believe that researchers share with others responsibility for the use to which findings are put and that this extends both the roles that researchers play and the skills they need (principles 5 and 6) (see Chapter 1, p. 5, Table 1.1).

In this chapter, we explore and illustrate some of the key decisions to be made about the production of research outputs. We start by considering internationally recognized theoretical models for the utilization of research and their implications for outputs. We then examine a series of issues raised by those models: the range of audiences to which study outputs should be communicated, forms of print and oral outputs and the use of a variety of media, including the role of 'new' technologies in communicating research findings. As in Chapters 5 and 6, we draw on a limited number of examples of our own experience, given not as models but as the basis for discussion. The main project we use in this chapter is a study of decision making within community-based multidisciplinary mental health teams, in shorthand, the 'Mental Health' study.

Research outputs: what works?

As we argued in Chapter 1, we have been struck by how narrow a concept of the completion of a research project is represented in textbooks written for students of research methods. This is despite both the extensive international literature about knowledge transfer, which tells a quite different story about the realities of research (Landry *et al.* 1998; Howard 2005; Sharp 2005), and the requirements of most research funders. For example, Matt Henn *et al.*'s (2005: 219) chapter on 'Writing Up and Presenting Research Results' begins:

> The culmination of a research project arrives when all the hard work is put to paper and the fruits of our labour are shared with a wider audience. This means writing up our research . . . The foundation for this approach to writing is that research projects do not exist in isolation, but contribute to a wider body of knowledge which is constantly developing.

The focus is on knowledge rather than change and on a linear process of writing and publishing findings. Even Clarissa White *et al.* (2003), who clearly recognize that research will be presented in different forms and at different times to a variety of audiences, focus on the process of constructing and representing the form and the nature of the phenomena that have been studied rather than on managing the impact of findings on those who hear about them. There is little or no discussion of reporting research data as an interactive process, as one involving power and influence or designed to produce change.

For much student research at undergraduate and postgraduate levels the primary purpose is passing the course and this usually requires a combination of oral and written presentations to a closed audience – perhaps only the tutor.

For some paid university-based researchers too, the focus of reporting may be on the academic community and this can be reinforced by measures of the quality of research that equate 'impact factors' with citations by other academics. However, for most research carried out by paid researchers, writing up is only a stage in a larger process of making findings known to a wider public. Sometimes, funders will require that research is kept confidential (and this can cause significant ethical, practical and other issues for researchers), but usually a major purpose of research is to draw wider attention to an issue which the commissioners or funders believe to be of importance. For commissioners or funders, the desire to secure value for money means that there is an increasing concern with the utilization of research, with whether the investment in research produces a return in terms of policy or practice change and/ or commercial exploitation. For example, the Joseph Rowntree Foundation is explicit in saying that it 'seeks to fund research and development which has the capacity to change policy or practice for the better. It does not fund the pursuit of knowledge for its own sake' (JRF 2006).

The issue of what works in enhancing the use to which research is put has itself been the focus of research over many decades. Rejean Landry *et al.* (1998) report on a study of social science research utilization in Canada carried out in the 1990s. Reviewing evidence about what makes research likely to be used, they identified six broad categories and then asked a large sample of social scientists to rate their relevance to utilization. The following factors were thought to affect utilization.

The types of research product: the 'science push' model of utilization suggests that the advancement of knowledge generated by research is seen as a key factor in utilization. Some argue that this favours quantitative over qualitative studies and this was supported for some but not for the practice-oriented social science disciplines (social work and industrial relations in this study).

The adaptation of products: factors linked to a dissemination (sic) model such as making reports more readable, conclusions and recommendations more specific, more operational and focusing on variables that users can influence were supported for both practice-oriented and other disciplines.

Dissemination efforts: here this refers to direct work with research users to discuss and present results and reflects an interactive model of utilization.

Linkage mechanisms: another element of interactivity, this factor includes a variety of kinds of contacts between researchers and users, including efforts such as participation in committees and personal contacts.

Users' context: refers to the value of making efforts to ensure that research is seen as pertinent by users, coincides with users' needs and is timely. This variable was the most strongly correlated with utilization in the study.

Researchers' context: this was difficult to operationalize but was assessed in terms of volume of publications, researchers' focus on the needs of users rather than on knowledge advancement and whether the source of funding was internal or external to universities, i.e. whether it required researchers to look outside in reporting findings. The results for this variable were equivocal. Paradoxically in view of the previous category, focusing on users' needs here did not correlate with utilization.

Despite the methodological limitations of the Canadian study, these elements and the delineation of different models for securing the use of research findings give a number of valuable clues to what researchers could be thinking about when assessing their strategy for producing outputs (and for influencing outcomes). Outputs are more likely to produce change when they reflect research evidence that is perceived to be of good quality about topics that are of current concern to end users, are well adapted for use, give clear guidance about implications for practice and are reported through a variety of interactive processes (Alkin 1985). These factors underpin the emphasis we place in the extending social research model on building and sustaining relationships with users and other interested stakeholders throughout the research process, on the importance of how research contracts are negotiated with funders to ensure that the focus of research fits with users' requirements (See Chapters 5 and 6) and on an approach to reporting that pays attention to processes of communication and the context into which messages are conveyed.

There is also the danger that research reports will be well received when or even because they do not offer a significant challenge to the pre-existing views held by the funders or other stakeholders. For example, Marvin Alkin (1985) argues that evaluators should limit their study to variables over which decision makers have some control. While this may make findings more likely to be implemented, it is scarcely ethical for researchers to ignore major issues because they cannot be immediately acted on. To study health inequalities for the UK National Health Service but to ignore the impact of poverty because it falls outside the brief of the Department of Health would be neither ethical nor sensible. Similarly, Peter Rossi and Howard Freeman (1993) argue that reports that respect stakeholders' existing programme commitments are more likely to lead to action on recommendations but, while this may be true, if programmes need to change for outcomes to improve then this advice is of limited value.

Many of these considerations about how to approach the production of research outputs are reflected in the 'Mental Health' study – the main example we are going to draw on in this chapter. The 'Mental Health' study was a project which aimed to examine the influence of different ways of thinking about serious mental health problems on shared decision making within community-based multidisciplinary mental health teams (Colombo *et al.* 2003, 2004; Fulford and Colombo 2004; Colombo forthcoming). In the study, one hundred respondents, representing five distinct multi-agency groups – psychiatrists, community psychiatric nurses, approved social workers, patients with schizophrenia and their families and relatives – operating within a specific mental health catchment area within England were asked their views regarding the treatment, management and care of people experiencing long-term schizophrenia.

Given the complex and potentially controversial nature of the subject matter under consideration it was felt from the outset that it would be valuable to establish an advisory research network. This network of research partners included representatives from regional mental health and social service organizations, academics with expertise and an interest in mental health matters, regional service user support groups such as MindLink, and various regional voluntary organizations working with service users and informal carers. An important function of this network was to ensure that the views of each multi-agency group participating in the research were fully represented across every aspect of the research project, particularly in terms of:

- generating the central purpose and rationale of the study;
- developing the research design and methods of implementation;
- organizing the reporting of the study's outputs; and
- considering of future outcomes.

The rationale for this strategy was that involvement of stakeholders from all of the participating groups would create common ownership of the project. In turn, this would enable the researchers to reduce the dominance of any one perspective in the research (and thus minimize potential bias), support access to research respondents and increase the likelihood that findings would influence future practice. Members of the network were involved in all stages of the project: writing the bid, the research design, securing access to respondents, and data analysis. The network also debated the strategy for presenting and publicising results.

Output strategy and audiences

As we have argued throughout (and particularly in Chapter 4), consideration of the output strategy is something which must initially be undertaken at the research design stage. There are two obvious principal reasons for this. The cost (including staff time) of producing outputs needs to be taken into account when a project budget is drawn up and negotiated. In addition to the amount of staff time involved, some kinds of outputs carry considerably more potential cost than others (full colour glossy reports widely distributed without charge versus publication via the internet). Some outputs carry a financial risk but may produce commercial value: for example, training materials or a national conference at which results will be presented. But, beyond cost, the kinds of outputs that can be produced will be affected by the forms of data gathering and analysis undertaken. For example, if a DVD is to be produced that includes interviews with research respondents, decisions have to be made about whether that material is obtained as part of the interview process. If photographs illustrating the progress of the project are to be included in the final report (as, for example, in Christine Milligan *et al.*'s (2003) study of therapeutic gardening), they have to be built into the process.

Target audiences

Before we can start to produce outputs from research it is important to understand something about the types and nature of the audiences to whom findings will be made available. Many of the studies of utilization emphasize the importance of identifying and understanding key decision makers and making them a target of an output strategy (Alkin 1985; Rossi and Freeman 1993; Monnier 1997). Perhaps because they are writing primarily about evaluations of service programmes, what those authors tend to focus on is the perspective and interests of the research commissioner. We would argue that researchers have a wider obligation to a variety of stakeholders. These will include several main groups (no priority implied):

- research respondents;
- organizational stakeholders:
  - policy makers;
  - managers;
  - service user and carer groups;
  - practitioners;
- communities of interest:
  - social movements;
  - professional bodies;
  - politicians;
  - academic and research communities;
- the public;
- funders (if different from the above).

Tony Colombo *et al.*'s 'Mental Health' study involved the five respondent populations detailed above. The organizational stakeholders included everyone belonging to each of these respective survey groups who worked or used services within the catchment area – the Mental Health Trust covered by the study. The implications of the study were likely to be of general interest to an extensive range of communities of interest, including anyone engaged in the community care of people with long-term schizophrenia, policy makers and the general public, and this needed to be reflected in the types of output that were produced.

Managing audience reception

Research outputs are read in context, by people who usually have prior commitments to the issues involved. Therefore, the output strategy needs to consider not only who the target audiences are but how that process of targeting will be made most effective. For each of the different populations who may be directly or indirectly affected by the outcomes of a study, a range of different reactions to the findings may occur. Some people or organizations may feel directly or indirectly criticized by the findings and recommendations and may be defensive, hesitant or sceptical about them. They may mount serious attempts to deflect or undermine the research itself. Others may be fascinated and have high, perhaps unrealistic, hopes that the research will make a difference to their lives and may expect to see results being turned into action. Others still may see the findings as a tool to promote their interests, whether or not they are directly relevant. These and other issues that affect how research is received can be actively managed by researchers, with greater or lesser success.

As noted in Chapter 6, and following the sustained interaction model, our approach to managing these issues has normally involved trying to build and retain close working relationships with interested parties throughout the research process. As also noted in Chapter 6, through the example of a project focusing on 'Institutional Racism', this does not always work because of the range of powerful factors in play.

In the 'Mental Health' study the diverse range of groups either directly or indirectly affected by the research presented particular challenges. For example, of the patient sample included in the study, only 50 per cent expressed an interest in being informed about the findings. Of those who expressed no interest, some seemed disillusioned. As one respondent put it: 'Whatever you come up with it probably won't make much difference anyway. I've been down this road before ... I only get involved because someone might take what we say seriously.' Some respondent psychiatrists were also quite defensive and concerned that the findings might portray them in a 'bad light'. Moreover, there was a degree of anxiety amongst some respondents from the patient group who felt that research outputs expressing their views might have a negative impact on the future quality of their treatment and care. There was also some concern within each practitioner group about the prospect that their views about other professions would be included as part of the research output. In fact, one of the key findings to be reported highlighted the existence of a considerable degree of conflict between psychiatrists and social workers.

One factor that helped to manage these tensions was the effort that had been put into the process of building the research network. Because different groups of respondents had been part of the research process from the outset they were in a position to make a meaningful contribution to the preparation and distribution of the study's final outputs. Involvement throughout helped to develop a sense of trust between the research team and the respondent populations, which was especially important given the professional, organizational and personal sensitivities involved.

Tailoring outputs to audiences

One element of 'audience management' involves considering the range of different abilities and resources people have for accessing knowledge. Only a minority of the audiences is likely to be used to and capable of dealing with information presented in a traditional academic style, while others may find more outcome-focused, factual or informal approaches more helpful. Some people will want to read the full background to how the findings were arrived at, and ethical researchers would want this to be the case, but many will want a short summary highlighting the action points or key findings. Moreover, researchers should consider the whole range of possible output media in deciding how best to reach their target audiences, an issue we return to shortly.

For Colombo *et al.*, in relation to the 'Mental Health' study, assessing how to tailor outputs to audiences was complex, given the diverse range of populations included in the study. For example, the advisory research network proposed that different forms of presentation of the research findings should be given to the mental health staff and to respondents who were patients with schizophrenia and their relatives. Attempts were made to ensure that the content and organization of any written outputs were designed to suit the perceived needs and interests of each particular population.

Enlisting intermediaries

In addition to partnerships with the key stakeholders involved in a particular project, researchers can engage with other groups and organizations in order to maximize the reach of their outputs. For example, some research funders will have their own systems for distributing research evidence. In the UK, the Joseph Rowntree Foundation 'Findings' series is a classic format to which every project they fund has to conform. The ESRC has established a 'Connect Club' to brief senior policy makers, which issues a regular newsletter, *The Edge*. Partnerships may also be developed with organizations concerned with informing practitioners about research evidence. Links with organizations such as Making Research Count (www.uea.ac.uk/swk/MRC_web/public_html/) and Research In Practice (www.rip.org.uk/) can provide ready-made avenues for informing a wide professional constituency about research findings. Generic or specific user-led groups and organizations such as Shaping Our Lives (www.shapingourlives.org.uk/index.htm) or Involve (www.invo.org.uk/) and quasi-representative organizations with a large contact base, such as Age Concern England or Mind, can also be targeted as effective intermediaries to widen the reach of findings. In the 'Mental Health' study, Mindlink played a significant role in publicizing findings to a national network of mental health service survivors. The British evidence-based practice organization, the Social Care Institute for Excellence, will pick up published literature and make it available through 'social care online' (www.scie-socialcareonline.org.uk/) but might not access grey literature unless it is brought to their attention.

Forms of output

Written outputs

Conventionally in research methods texts a small number of kinds of print-based outputs are the focus of attention: the thesis, the research report and, perhaps, articles for publication in peer-reviewed journals (see, for example, Effendi and Hamber 1999; Blaxter *et al.* 2001; Ritchie and Lewis 2003; Henn *et al.* 2005). These are outputs which primarily appeal to and are accessed by academically orientated audiences and these and other texts have some useful guidance about producing them. Here we will concentrate on issues associated with producing other kinds of outputs.

Put simply, the accessibility of findings involves two main interlocking dimensions: whether the target audience will see the materials and whether they will be able to read and understand them if they do. But a number of factors contribute to these core issues. To maximize access to outputs, several points need to be considered, one of which is producing results in a variety of formats. In addition to the traditional forms mentioned above, researchers often produce a range of other kinds of formats and styles of print output in order to make their findings more available, particularly to non-academic audiences. These may include one or more of the following:

- brief summary feedback sheets in written and electronic forms which can be distributed easily, placed on notice boards, entered on a website, etc.;
- executive summaries that concentrate on the key findings and recommendations;
- short articles for in-house newsletters or good practice journals;
- articles in local and national newspapers or special interest magazines;
- letters to local and national newspapers or special interest magazines;
- good practice guides aimed at professional audiences;
- brief 'self-help' advice sheets aimed at lay audiences;
- training packages which include the research findings as part of a larger development process.

Of course, some of these formats arguably move beyond being just reports of research to being an outcome, part of the process of applying and implementing the findings.

Providing access to findings is not just a matter of whether appropriate materials are produced but also how effectively they are distributed to the target audiences outlined above. Maximizing accessibility may well require a different distribution strategy for each of the selected audiences (Shanley *et al.* 1996). Using existing, well tried distribution systems, such as in-house or professional journals, backed up by full reports available through the net may work for some groups. If materials have to be purchased, cost can be a barrier. It would be of little use targeting a group which did not have ready access to the internet through web-based materials. If the web is a primary means of distribution researchers have to alert potential readers to the existence of the web file and this may again require carefully tailored strategies.

Ideally outputs will become available at a relevant time when potential recipients will be motivated to read and act upon them. This is one reason why relatively quick updates of research may have more impact than a polished full report produced months after the conclusion of a project. Timing can, of course, also be used to suppress breadth of access, as we exemplified in Chapter 5.

The language used in research reports can be a further barrier to the accessibility of findings (Carroll *et al.* 1997). All too rarely are the outcomes of research or information signposting people to research reports made available in languages other than English, using Braille or in large print for people with sight impairments or in easy to read formats for people with learning disabilities, although examples are found. The UK government has some good examples of producing documents in easy to read format, for example, a version of the *Choosing Health* white paper is available at www.dh.gov.uk/assetRoot/04/09/51/65/04095165.pdf. Some useful guidance for producing easy to read materials can be found on the Medline Plus website of the US National Library of Health and the National Institutes of Health (www.nlm.nih.gov/medlineplus/etr.html). Mencap also has a useful guide to accessibility generally, including making written materials accessible, which is available at www.mencap.co.uk/html/accessibility/accessibility_guides.htm.

The 'Mental Health' study produced several different print outputs in order to reach the range of audiences associated with the study. These included academic papers; articles for practice-based magazines that would appeal to a range of mental health and social service professionals and patients; short information pieces that were included in newsletters distributed to its members through MindLink and information fact sheets that were sent to all the study's respondents. These fact sheets were organized around a summary of the study, a 'thank you for participation' and then a short bullet point extract of the key findings written in plain English with the intention that it would be widely accessible. In addition to this standardized element, a separate information sheet was included that contained research output that related specifically to each respondent population. The findings were also used by the Sainsbury Centre to develop a training package on shared decision making in community mental health teams. This package was used to train mental health and social service practitioners across the UK and so ensured further coverage for the findings.

There are considerable time and resource implications associated with trying to produce such a range of outputs. However, in the 'Mental Health' study this was partly overcome by getting the various groups associated with the advisory network involved in the production and distribution of printed outputs. For example, staff of various mental health voluntary groups took on the responsibility of organizing the research findings into a style and format that would be more accessible to their members. Given their skills and experience in working with people with mental health problems, it seemed obvious to the research team that they should take over responsibility for presenting the findings. This option helped spread the workload and would probably not have been available without the existence of the advisory network. However, it is questionable whether this transfer of costs is always appropriate, especially as many representative voluntary, self-help and user groups have limited funding. Hence, a realistic budget for the production of accessible materials should be built into project costing and ring-fenced.

Oral presentations and outputs

The second conventional academic form of research outputs in addition to journal articles is through presenting papers at conferences or seminars. As with written reports, there are numerous sources of standard guidance for making oral presentations. 'Effective Presentations' is just one (www.kumc. edu/SAH/OTEd/jradel/effective.html). However, a variety of other methods of oral presentation are also available but rarely mentioned in the literature. These include verbal reporting back to funders, respondents and other stakeholders through a variety of kinds of meeting from one-to-ones, advisory groups and committees to large public events. Moreover, for any given setting there are a variety of ways of enhancing the impact of presentations, not just by the use of the ubiquitous powerpoint software but also through drama, song and other forms, perhaps using radio, television or film, DVD, video, audio tape or CDs. The media dimensions of oral presentations are discussed later.

As with print-based outputs, the strategy chosen needs to be based on an analysis of the audiences it is intended to reach, the consequent value of different kinds of presentation, the factors that will maximize whatever impact is desired, and considerations such as format, timing, language and style.

As the 'Mental Health' study was primarily concerned with the issue of multi-agency working, it was felt appropriate to set up a seminar presentation and invite all the groups involved in the study, both respondents and other members of staff, service users and carers. The seminar was very successful in attracting psychiatrists, psychiatric nurses and social workers working within the catchment area, with over 60 attending. However, patients and informal carers were also invited but only one respondent attended. This was anticipated and so small groups were also organized through local voluntary organizations. These groups were open to all patient and carer members in the region. These proved to be much more successful, and resulted in an open exchange of views about the findings. In fact, it was unusual for members of these organizations to get together in such a way. As a result, an informal carers' group was established to discuss and provide support to each other regarding their common problems and concerns. The presentations to patients and informal carers were much more informal than they had been for practitioners, and the groups were small enough (usually around 10 members) for respondents and other service users and carers to feel more confident about asking questions and contributing an opinion.

One of the challenges that was not overcome was an attempt to create a forum in which the results could have been discussed between representatives from both the professional and patients' groups. Furthermore, although the research appears to have gone some way towards creating a greater sense of common identity between professionals and patients, the lack of time and general resources prevented this from being developed further. The production of the training materials might help in the future.

Another aspect associated with publicizing findings through oral presentations is that it enabled the research team to involve groups of people that conventional approaches have often failed to reach in the past. For example, there was a particular group of patients with schizophrenia involved in the study that experienced considerable difficulties in trusting and generally engaging with support services. Respondents from this group did not feel able to attend the focus groups that were set up and so their key workers were asked to discuss the findings with these respondents during their one-to-one meetings. This approach demonstrates the value of flexibility and a targeted access strategy in reaching groups normally excluded from the process.

The 'Hate Crime' project (Allender and Quigley 2005) was another study undertaken by the Centre for Social Justice (CSJ) and commissioned by a local authority, focusing on gathering evidence of reporting people's first-hand experience of hate crime. In reporting the study, a conference was held which was designed to attract a wide range of paid staff from a variety of local organizations, local councillors, volunteers and members of the general public. This was a project with a high level of participation in which members of groups who were subject to hate crime had been recruited to carry out most of the interviewing. Rather than give a conventional presentation to the conference it was decided to use more interactive methods with a view to making the findings more accessible to a wide 'lay' audience. In addition to producing research findings in the form of a CD-ROM, and oral presentations shared by university-based researchers and those trained locally, a local drama group was employed to turn the findings into a play. Throughout the day, people attending the conference were encouraged to respond in discussion and by writing thoughts and proposed actions on post-it notes, which were displayed on the wall. This created a more engaged atmosphere than would otherwise have been the case. However, the drama was felt by the research team to have poorly represented the findings of the study and with hindsight it was felt that much more control should have been exercised over both how the findings were translated into a dramatic script and the quality of the production. Undoubtedly, care has to be taken to exercise quality control when research findings are publicized second-hand in this way.

Technology and outputs

As new forms of information technology have become available they are forming an increasingly large role in the production and distribution of research outputs. The internet is now many academics' most common form of access to journal articles and other forms of web-based publications identified through databases and search engines. This has led to global debates about whether web hits could replace other measures as indicators of productivity and esteem for academics (Smith and Thelwall 2002).

These changes have shifted, and continue to affect, the relative value of different kinds of output for reaching and influencing different audiences. David Dickson (2001) – amongst others – has argued that the internet has the capacity to revolutionize relationships between academic researchers and the public through making research widely available and providing a medium for dialogue. Lesley Grayson and Alan Gomersall (2003) suggest that systematic reviews in social science have been made more difficult because of the range and volume of new material to access and problems in assessing quality when including work which has not been peer reviewed.

The internet provides new opportunities for publicizing results and making research accessible, but some of the same concerns that apply to print media and oral presentations remain equally relevant. Researchers (working with other stakeholders) need to ask the same questions about who can be reached – and who is excluded – by online publication. Similarly, the format, style and language in which materials are presented remain important. For example, the accessibility of web materials to disabled people needs to be considered (guidance from the Disability Rights Commission can be found on www.drc-gb.org/publicationsandreports/report.asp). But the fundamental problem – globally – is that differential access to information technology is currently increasing the inequalities in access to knowledge and information that have always existed.

Despite this, there can be little doubt about the potential power of this approach to make outputs widely available to the general public as well as academic and professional audiences, although there is less evidence about its impact on policy making or practice. One small study of self-harm conducted by researchers from the CSJ from 2000 to 2002 for the children's charity NCH was published in print form both as a full report (Bywaters and Rolfe 2002) and in summary (eight-page) form, and a short leaflet giving advice to people who knew someone who self-harmed was also produced. These materials were also made available on the charity's website (www.nch.org.uk/information/

index.php?i=136) and – in conjunction with a media campaign of which more later – this resulted in over 50,000 copies of one or other form of output (mostly the full report) being downloaded within the first year. This size of readership vastly exceeded anything generated by journal or even professional magazine articles.

The 'Mental Health' study used online newsletters in order to gain wider circulation for findings. These pages were accessible not only to local members of a particular population, but anyone else who had access to the world wide web and was interested in the study. In a development of the study being conducted by email, email and the internet will also be used as the key methods for informing respondents about the research findings.

Media and outputs

Social scientists have long had a cautious approach to using the communications media (newspapers, TV, radio) to publicize research. For example, Helen Roberts in 1984 was discussing the 'politics of the popularisation of research findings' (Roberts 1994: 199). Despite cautionary tales about the distortion of research by the media, Roberts clearly believed that making social science research popularly available is important for three main reasons:

- responsibility to respondents;
- to enhance the credibility of the social sciences; and
- because of the potential impact on elite audiences of pressure from 'below'.

Once again, the fundamental issues of strategy remain similar. Considerations of audience, format, access, timing and language remain important and decisions about what the ESRC (2006a) calls the communication strategy should still be made in conjunction with other stakeholders. What is new is a further range of written and oral skills, which are required for writing press releases or newspaper articles or for presenting research findings on news bulletins or phone-in, discussion or documentary programmes. For many researchers, handling the popular media involves little-known skills, despite the efforts of the ESRC to ensure that media training is built into postgraduate research programmes and in publishing good practice guides (Gaber 2001; Vaitilingam 2001) and a Communications Toolkit (ESRC 2006).

This involves a further set of relationships for researchers to consider developing. The ESRC's (2006b) '10 Top Tips in Media Relations' emphasizes the value of long-term relationships with journalists as a way of managing the production of media outputs based on research as well as other ways of controlling the process of news making.

The cautionary tales about social scientists' engagement with the media mainly concern the distortion of findings and the exposure of individuals, both researchers and respondents, by the shorthand and personalized approach sometimes taken. It is not just that publicizing research through the media involves loss of control; researchers never control how their messages are read or heard or interpreted, in whatever media they are produced (Alvesson 2002). In one study in our experience (Colombo and Neary 1998), the media made life for the research team very difficult indeed. The study in question was on the development of statistical risk assessment measures which attempted to predict the likelihood of someone reoffending within two years. The project was initially funded by the Home Office and their intention was that the statistical measure be used by magistrates as a guide to determining whether or not to give an offender a prison sentence. If their risk of reoffending was predicted to be high, this might be used as a justification for imprisonment. Not surprisingly, the probation service was displeased at this prospect and voiced their concerns to several national newspapers. The impact was to completely alter the course of the study towards looking at probation officers' anxieties about the use of such statistical measures. On the other hand, the 'Young Parents' research team has been encouraged by the positive coverage of their work concerned with the support agenda within the Teenage Pregnancy Strategy, as support for young parents is often framed in local and national media as supporting promiscuity.

It is important to make every effort to anticipate negative as well as positive responses to research at the outset, especially when researching high-profile subjects that are likely to prove controversial and so attract the interest of the media. Working through a good press office, as we did with the 'Young Parents' project, is invaluable.

End points

In this chapter we have looked at some of the decisions that have to be made about how to publish and publicize research findings. We have argued that focusing on utilization carries a set of strategic and tactical decisions that are ideally mapped out at the start of the project because of the importance of building them into the design and costing. We are suggesting, by implication, that an inadequate proportion of research funding has usually been allocated to this stage of the process. Producing accessible outputs for a wide audience is a time-consuming and costly business. Moreover, other factors affecting researchers' organizational contexts and careers will also influence this process. The urge to secure the next grant or write the RAE publication will often weigh more heavily than extensive publication and discussion of findings with interested parties and wider publics. But the production of outputs is only part of this process of extending social research. Influencing outcomes is also part of the process, as we shall discuss in the next chapter.

8

Outcomes

Geraldine Brady, Paul Bywaters, Mary Knyspel,
Gayle Letherby and Graham Steventon

*Introduction • Arguments against a close relationship between research
and practice • Key issues • What works? • Opportunities and barriers
• End points*

Introduction

Extending social researchers' responsibility from outputs to outcomes – to the
application and implementation of research findings – is a complex and a
contentious issue. It is contentious both because some argue that this is not
part of the researcher's role, indeed that research is damaged by too close a
relationship with implementation (Gray 2004) and because the application
and implementation of research findings is not a linear process but involves
a series of political and personal decisions and commitments. It is complex
because the processes through which research comes to have an impact
on practice and policy making are multifaceted, with issues of power and
resistance central considerations.

Because most research methods' texts scarcely mention the role of researchers in turning findings into social change, once again in this chapter we
will be drawing primarily on literature which focuses on research utilization,
evidence-based practice or knowledge transfer. These different terms have
overlapping content and are more or less widely used in different disciplines.

The concept of knowledge transfer is found more frequently in management and organizational literature (for example, Eliasson 1996; Argote and Ingram 2000) and is more likely to be focused on the commercial exploitation of research findings either by universities or academics acting alone or – more commonly – through partnerships between universities and commercial organizations. It was the central concept in the Lambert Review of Business–University Collaboration (HM Treasury 2003) that contributed to a major re-think of UK government funding for research and innovation. The concepts of research utilization and evidence-based practice are more widely used in the policy and practice worlds of education, health and social care (e.g. Walter *et al.* 2004a; French 2005; Jones and Santaguida 2005).

Whichever concept is used, they imply a model of the research and practice worlds as being 'two communities' (Caplan 1979; Fox 2003) – or the three communities of research, policy and practice (Locock and Boaz 2004). The motivation for ensuring that research findings have an impact is seen as either concerned with 'push' or 'pull' factors. That is to say, either concerned with the efforts of researchers to secure a response from practitioners and policy makers or the efforts of the practitioners and policy makers to obtain useful knowledge to inform their decisions and actions. As we suggested in Chapter 7, 'pushing information from the centre out is insufficient and often ineffective: we also need to develop strategies that encourage a "pull" for information from potential end users', whether those are service providers or service users (Nutley *et al.* 2002: 6). For example, in recent times we have seen the power of patients who have used research evidence about the benefits of new drugs, such as the cancer treatment Herceptin, to influence health policy in the UK. These push and pull factors are sometimes directly apparent in the contracts established between commissioners and researchers but also appear indirectly in the relationships between researchers and other funders such as the ESRC or JRF in the UK. As we have written earlier, these funders, like commissioners, are increasingly concerned to get an unambiguous return for investment in the form of practically useful findings.

In this chapter, we explore the roles that researchers can play in turning findings into outcomes. We draw mainly on examples from our 'Young Parent' projects first introduced in Chapter 5, but also include references to two other Centre for Social Justice (CSJ) projects, concerning looked after children and hate crime (introduced in Chapter 7). In a sense, all six of our principles come into play in this chapter as it is the focus on impact (principle 1) or outcomes which underpins the whole approach of extending social research. There is a particular emphasis here on the extended roles for researchers (principle 5) who get involved in the processes of application and implementation, while the skills required are discussed in more detail in the following chapter (see Chapter 1, p. 5, Table 1.1). What emerges constitutes, to an extent, a critique of the binary divide between researcher and practitioner or researcher and policy maker, implicit in the 'two communities' model referred to above, and support for Nick Fox's (2003) proposition that research is itself a form of human practice on a continuum with other kinds of activity rather than an inherently different and separate activity based on a superior ability to represent truth.

Arguments against a close relationship between research and practice

Before we consider the complexities of researchers' tasks in engaging with the application and implementation of their findings, we need to discuss a number of prior issues, the first of which is the arguments for and against such a focus on outcomes. We have argued that there are a number of reasons for this close engagement including the view that change is the primary purpose of social science research, that ethical commitments to respondents, research funders and wider populations demand a focus on outcomes and that research itself is strengthened because findings are validated or changed and developed by what is learnt from implementation.

However, there are also strongly held counter-arguments. The main objection is that such an emphasis on outcomes is liable to undermine the value of research. The very processes that enhance the chances of research making a difference may also undermine its contribution by linking researchers too closely to research users for them to be able to play an independent role. As we shall discuss later, evidence suggests that direct personal contact and producing recommendations that policy makers find confirm current thinking are correlated with better chances of research being applied. These are undoubtedly a threat to researchers' ability to think and report independently and are liable to lead to compromises in what is reported and recommended. As Simon Innvaer and colleagues (2002: 242) put it: 'If what is required for research to be used is that researchers do what the policy-maker wants them to do, then research may fail to fulfil one of its most important functions, namely to be objective, reliable and unbiased.' While we do not believe that researchers can be objective or unbiased, the relationship between the process and the product(s) should be transparent (see Chapter 3) and the product(s) should not be predetermined by either the funder or research end-user. The thin line between a productive collaboration between researchers and commissioners or funders and undue influence is sometimes hard to discern. At a deeper level, Jane Ritchie and Liz Spencer (1994) highlight the dangers that arise for social research if 'positivist' (see Chapter 1) approaches to methodology and policy makers' concern about discovering 'facts' dominate the way research is shaped and the outcomes derived from it. Adherence to traditional scientific methods and approaches because of a false belief that they can give unequivocal and direct solutions to political and practical problems produces both bad and dangerous social science.

A parallel concern has also been raised about whether increasing the use of research could have negative rather than positive outcomes for practice. Kieran Walshe and Thomas Rundall (2001) suggest that overuse (when tentative or poorly evidenced findings spread rapidly) and misuse (especially where evidence is ambiguous) of research can occur. And it is also the case that research – or even the process of setting up research programmes – can be used to block or deflect pressure for change or produce inappropriate change because of the questions that are posed.

These are all concerns based on a mistrust of policy makers and practitioners. They imply doubts about whether policy makers and practitioners have a sufficiently sophisticated understanding of research and ethical stance on the use of evidence to be trusted not to distort either the research process or the implementation of findings. As such, the arguments exemplify the 'two communities' perspective. We think these are arguments to be taken seriously. But we do not agree that they are grounds for researchers to relinquish all responsibility for outcomes, simply to drop their reports on the doormat of policy-making and service-provider organizations and leave. On the contrary, we would argue that they strengthen the case for close working relationships – for bridging the divide – not only in order to strengthen implementation but in order that research is carried out ethically: with the greatest possible honesty about what is sought and what can be achieved through research.

Key issues

A number of further issues also need some clarification. First, despite the emphasis placed in the previous chapter on communicating the findings of research, a word of caution is appropriate. We cannot expect there to be a one-to-one relationship between research and policy making or research and practice, even in an ideal world (Nutley et al. 2002). Policy makers have to consider not only evidence about what works, if it exists, but also political constraints and public attitudes. According to Janet Lewis (2001), the knowledge which practitioners in social care should draw on is made up of a combination of research evidence plus practice wisdom plus service user and carer experiences and wishes. Moreover, as Sandra Nutley et al. (2002: 4) argue, in many areas of public policy 'the research base is dominated by small, ad hoc studies, often diverse in approach and of dubious methodological quality. In consequence there is little accumulation from this research of a robust knowledge base'.

Second, what is meant by the 'use' of research is not straightforward. For example, different kinds of research will have very different kinds of relationships to policy and practice. Isabel Walter et al.'s (2004b) review of self-report studies suggests that research is used in both practice and policy making to:

- provide a foundation for restructuring services;
- inform policy and practice reviews and development work;
- address specific issues (problem solving);
- support a policy stance or argument;
- promote reasoned debate;
- assist with service monitoring and review;
- provide quality assurance;
- safeguard or justify funding.

In addition, research is used in policy making to inform:

- care standards;
- occupational standards;
- educational and training requirements.

The diversity of this list has implications for the design of research projects, which needs to be appropriate to the kinds of outcomes which are sought as well as the nature of the evidence that is required.

The Centre for Social Justice (CSJ) has been involved recently in two parallel pieces of work. One was an evaluation of a special programme in a single local authority area to improve the quality of life of looked after children and their involvement in decisions affecting their lives, both individually and at a policy level. On the face of it, at least, the evaluation was designed to ask fairly direct questions about which elements of the project, if any, should be continued and, if so, how they should be funded. Our recommendations were also relatively direct. A second project has looked at the subjective experience of hate crime (see Chapter 7) and was developed as a backdrop to decision making rather than having a direct relationship to it. It was designed to raise awareness of the existence and nature of hate crime, to inform both decision makers and a wider public, rather than to produce recommendations about particular actions. Jill Blackmore and Hugh Lauder (2005) make a distinction between research about policy and research for policy. The 'Looked After Children' project was directly for policy making, while the 'Hate Crime' project was concerned with the impact of current policies (or lack of policies) on people's lives.

Three types of research use or utilization are often identified in the literature. Peter Rossi and Howard Freeman (1993) and Innvaer and colleagues (2002) describe these as follows.

- Direct, instrumental or engineering – referring to findings used to make observable changes in the way a programme operates. May be partial or incremental implementation.
- Enlightening or conceptual – referring to research that affects how people think about a programme, helps establish new goals, enriches and deepens understanding of the complexity of problems and unintended consequences of action.

- Selective, persuasive, symbolic or legitimating – referring to the strategic use of research to legitimate and sustain, or to challenge, predetermined positions.

Nutley *et al.* (2002) divide the last type into two: involving the mobilization of support and securing wider influence on a particular issue. Of course, research can have relevance for more than one kind of use and, as Innvaer *et al.* (2002) point out, different kinds of use may vary according to the type of decision maker, type of policy question, and different issues. Our 'Looked After Children' research project had a *direct* relationship to policy and practice decisions, but was also *selective* in that, for some of the actors at least, there was a concern to legitimize work which had temporary funding as part of a process to achieve mainstream funding. It was also an opportunity to *enlighten* some of the decision makers about the experiences and requirements of looked after children. In addition, by adopting a participatory process involving young people, its methods sought to reinforce an approach to user involvement in decision making that was a key value position of the programme. The 'Hate Crime' project was relevant to both the legitimation of existing hate crime work and developing awareness of the complexities of the issues involved amongst a wide-reaching audience.

A third key issue is whether the same factors are at work in the relationship between research and policy making as for research and practice. There may be substantial overlap but the two fields are not coterminous. This is apparent in the evidence that, while policy sets the context for practice, policy makers have difficulty in ensuring that the policy intentions result in the anticipated practice outcomes and are not resisted, distorted or filleted (see Ladwig 1994).

Fourth, it cannot be assumed that either policy makers or practitioners are homogeneous, so that the same methods would work in all circumstances with each group. Frequently the description of 'practitioner' is used to cover a whole range of roles from a junior member of frontline staff, perhaps with few qualifications, through experienced professionals with degree-level education, to managers at different levels. Their capacity for understanding, degree of control over their own work and that of others and their interests in changing what is done vary considerably, and targeted change must consider the nature of the audience, as we discussed in Chapter 7. Nutley *et al.* (2002) found that the most effective strategies for ensuring research utilization were multifaceted and explicitly targeted barriers to change. Nothing works with all of the people all of the time. Change efforts have to be tailored to particular circumstances (NHS CRD 1999). Nutley *et al.* (2002: 9) concluded that 'the relationships between research, knowledge, policy and practice are always likely to remain loose, shifting and contingent'.

What works?

Nevertheless, there is some evidence about the factors that may make research more likely to influence policy and practice. Nutley and colleagues (2002) suggest that there are four requirements if evidence is to have a greater impact on policy and practice:

- agreement about what counts as evidence in what circumstances;
- a strategic approach to the creation of evidence in priority areas, with concomitant systematic efforts to accumulate evidence in the form of robust bodies of knowledge;
- effective dissemination of evidence to where it is most needed and the development of effective means of providing wide access to knowledge;
- initiatives to ensure the integration of evidence into policy and encourage the utilization of evidence in practice.

These issues are, of course, only partly in the hands of researchers. The first point is exemplified by the study of hate crime. The local authority chief executive was unimpressed by the study as evidence on which to base action because it was a qualitative study unable to quantify the scale or trend of the problem. This mismatch of expectations powerfully affected the reception of the study by a key decision maker, but may only have been the symptom of more fundamental differences of interest between researchers who wished to promote the more conflictually based hate crime approach to community relations and a manager who was more interested in action exemplifying the concept of community cohesion. Where research is commissioned at one level of an organization but is hoped to influence policy making at another level – as in this case – there is a potential for the research to meet one set of expectations but not the other, if this is not clarified in advance. Similarly, it can be difficult to ensure that all stakeholders in research conducted for multi-agency commissioners are starting from the same perceptions of issues such as 'what counts as evidence'.

Both Nutley *et al.* (2002) and Innvaer and colleagues (2002) from systematic reviews of the literature identify a very similar list of factors that make research findings more likely to be applied although the issues are expressed a little differently. Nutley *et al.*'s (2002: 17) list of factors relevant to both practitioners and policy makers is as follows:

a The research is timely, the evidence is clear and relevant, and the methodology is relatively uncontested.
b Results support existing ideologies, are convenient and uncontentious to the powerful.
c Policy makers believe in evidence as an important counterbalance to expert opinion, and act accordingly.

d The research findings have strong advocates.
e Research users are partners in the generation of evidence.
f Results are robust in implementation.
g Implementation is reversible if needs be.

Innvaer *et al.* (2002) – focusing exclusively on policy makers – find the strongest evidence for the importance of personal contact between researchers and policy makers, a particular version of the partnership concept that perhaps reflects the methodologies of the studies included, which were all based on interviews with policy makers. This was also reflected in the factors they found to be the most frequently mentioned barriers to implementation:

h Absence of personal contact.
i Lack of timeliness or relevance.
j Mutual mistrust including perceived political naivety of scientists and scientific naivety of policy makers.
k Power and budget struggles.
l Poor quality of research.
m Political instability or high turnover of policy-making staff.

(Innvaer 2002: 241)

It is useful to reflect, once again, on the 'Young Parent' research in relation to these factors. These projects have all been commissioned since 2001 by local Teenage Pregnancy Partnership Boards (TPPB) in five local areas led either by local authority or Primary Care Trust staff (factors c and e). As detailed in Chapter 5, measures to address teenage pregnancy and young parenthood were key priorities for the UK government during this period and targets were set which required inter-agency action incorporating both local authorities and the NHS (through the PCT) (factor b). In this sense the research was timely and, because commissioned by the body with responsibility for implementation, the methodology was uncontested (factor a). Projects were carried out in ways that closely involved the lead staff of the key organizations (factor e). As they also involved young pregnant women and young parents themselves that further strengthened the ideological support available to the projects (factor b). The incorporation of members of the research team into the Teenage Pregnancy Boards, and their membership and chairing of sub-committees, further strengthened the partnership basis of the research.

The commitment of both the commissioners and the researchers to applying and implementing findings led to a range of outcomes being achieved. One issue that emerged from the first project in this area – 'Supported Semi-Independent Housing for Under 18 Lone Parents: Needs Assessment' (Letherby *et al.* 2001), outlined in Chapter 5 – which was of particular concern, was young women's maternity experiences. Young women in this study spoke of negative ante-natal, birth and postnatal experiences and it became clear that because of negative encounters with health professionals and other pregnant women and their partners they did not always access the services that they were entitled to. Dissatisfaction with maternity services in the UK has a long history and is not restricted to young women (Thomas 1998) and in response to this there have been some recent positive developments. For example, the *Changing Childbirth* report (DoH 1993) recommends that the childbearing woman should be fully involved in choosing her care and should be enabled to feel involved and empowered (Weaver 2000). However, although the implication of this is that pregnant women themselves inform maternity services both Thomas (1998) and Weaver (2000) detail remaining tensions. As part of the government's aim to reduce health inequalities (including reducing infant mortality), the *National Service Framework for Children* (DoH 2004) identifies the need for improved access to antenatal and maternity services. This is alongside policy developments in health and social care which place a responsibility on Primary Care Trusts to provide appropriate and accessible services for young parents. Yet, we were anxious that given the prejudicial attitudes displayed by some professionals and others and the resultant lack of adequate preparation for birth and motherhood, it is likely that young parents find it particularly difficult to be 'fully involved' in the way that these documents advocate. This is reiterated in the publication *Teenage Parents: Who Cares?*, which details how young parents experience poorer access to maternity services and how this has implications both for their own health and well-being and that of their child/children (Teenage Pregnancy Unit *et al.* 2004).

Coventry TPPB were keen to respond to the concerns about maternity services that we raised in our 2001 report and in conjunction with Walsall TPPB asked us to write a proposal concerned to explore the pregnancy and post-natal experience of young women who become pregnant under the age of 20. This we did and were funded to undertake a project across the two regions in 2002 (Letherby *et al.* 2002). Again using qualitative methods – in-depth single and focus group interviews – we spoke to 38 young mothers, seven grandmothers and 49 professionals. Our key findings were as follows.

- There are myths and stereotypes on both sides, i.e. both professionals and young people hold stereotypes about each other *but* professionals have more power and, therefore, the stereotypes they hold are more significant.
- With reference to contraceptive use, young people (especially girls or young women) are 'damned if they do and damned if they don't', as contraceptive use defines a girl or young woman as sexually active and 'looking for sex' and lack of contraceptive use marks a girl or young woman as irresponsible.
- Contrary to popular myth, some of the babies of teenagers are planned and certainly for the young women we spoke to all babies were wanted.
- Encounters with professionals are often structured by misunderstandings and frustration, which means that access to services is non-existent or meaningless.

- Young women have a largely negative experience of birth and maternity services.
- Overall, teenage pregnancy and young motherhood is structured by power and control – within professional and personal relationships.

Following on from our findings we concluded the project with several recommendations for policy and future research. These included:

Awareness raising – both health professionals and young women need help to challenge the dominant negative discourses of teenage pregnancy. Whilst recognizing the importance of making young women aware of their possible current and future reproductive choices, 'support' needs to be just that and health professionals need to be careful not to appear judgemental by focusing on prevention. As well as ongoing training for health professionals and sessions that provide young women with the opportunity to share their concerns and experiences in a non-judgemental environment, joint focus group work with professionals and young women may encourage the process of 'listening' and alleviate frustration on both sides.

Specialist services – our data suggest that targeted services, both ante- and post-natal, organized *at appropriate times*, in *accessible, non-threatening* locations and focusing on the particular concerns of young women would be accessed. Some young women need one-to-one as well as group support.

Designated midwives and health visitors – specialist training for a sub-set of health professionals needs to include not only the above awareness training but knowledge of the practical concerns and the specific emotional and medical needs of young pregnant women/mothers. These key professionals would not only provide young women with access to expert advice and continuity of care but the good practice of these individuals would influence the practice of all.

(Letherby *et al.* 2002: 41)

As a result of these recommendations Coventry TPPB:

- established a Young Parents' Forum;
- commissioned the CSJ to design and deliver a training programme for health and social care professionals which was produced and presented by the research team that worked on the 2002 project with the help of young mothers;
- secured funding for specialist services aimed at addressing the ante- and post-natal needs of pregnant teenagers and young parents (aged 16–24) in Coventry for an initial period of two years.

In order to demonstrate further the involvement of the research team in non-traditional outcomes we focus briefly on the Training Programme and the Specialist Services.

Young parents: training programme

Again, our suggestions for further action were taken up by the commissioners of the research. The training, which included pilot and full development stages, took two years to develop. The aims of the training are:

- to raise awareness of the experience of pregnant teenagers and young parents;
- to enable professionals to challenge and change their own practice and those of colleagues;
- to enable professionals to help pregnant teenagers and young parents to challenge their own stereotypes and those of others;
- to encourage reflexive practice.

The training takes place over two days, one month apart. It is supported by training materials developed out of the research including:

- storyboards of the holistic experience of young parents (using narrative and photographs from young people);
- a video or DVD (*Listening to Young Parents*), which includes young mothers talking about their experience and scenarios drawn from the data including young parents as actors.

In addition the training includes various group discussions and exercises and the keeping of a practice diary between the first and second sessions.

At the beginning of the first session professionals are asked to keep the following issues in mind:

- the need to work towards an holistic view of teenage pregnancy and young parenthood that recognizes:
  - the importance of support within the Teenage Pregnancy Strategy;
  - the importance of a focus on the positive as well as the negative aspects of teenage pregnancy and young parenthood.

They are reminded that:

- Parenthood needs to be viewed as a legitimate transition, a legitimate 'rite of passage' for young men and women.

(Letherby *et al.* 2004: 58)

- The tendency to approach teenage pregnancy as a social problem has led to an exaggeration of negative outcomes and resulted in the positive aspects of teenage parenthood being ignored.

    (Bunting and McAuley 2004: 208)

- Overall the provision of support had a stronger relationship to maternal well-being than any other independent variable, confirming the importance of such support for all teenage mothers.

    (Bunting and McAuley 2004: 209)

The production and presentation of the training has been a positive experience for the research team, not least because of the involvement of young women. At the development stage, young women were involved in the production of story boards which involved further interviews, this time with photographic work (either choosing existing photographs or taking new ones); the making of the video/DVD which involved the filming of two discussion groups and five short scenarios, enacted by young women and men and members of the CSJ. An example of this, along with the introductory comments/instructions is given below:

Scenarios

The events outlined here all actually happened and appear in a somewhat different form in the reports of our research. The scenarios are drawn largely from Letherby *et al.* (2002) but to a lesser extent from other projects that we have undertaken. However, sometimes we have drawn on more than one/several experiences for dramatic effect.

After you have watched/read each one of the following scenarios consider the following questions:

1   What is actually happening here? What good and bad practice can you identify? What stereotypes and prejudices does this highlight?
2   Does this remind you of any incidents you have been involved in/observed/heard about?
3   What challenges does this present for your practice?
4   How might you challenge the stereotypes and prejudice outlined here?
5   In what ways could you intervene to encourage young pregnant women and young mothers to challenge the prejudices and discrimination they face?

SCENARIO TWO – 'What do you want her to do about it?'

SCENE ONE: A doctor and a midwife are talking together during a coffee break.

Doctor [reading the newspaper]: 'Have you read this article about the rise in teenage pregnancy? It's just shocking isn't it? It's because they don't act responsibly you know, sleep with boys on the first date and don't bother with contraceptives, I blame the parents myself tut tut tut.'

Midwife: 'Don't you think that's a little short sighted, I mean these young women are damned if they do and damned if they don't. If they get pregnant we call them irresponsible, if they use contraceptives we call them promiscuous and I know they have to deal with prejudice on the street (one of my young patients told me recently that a guy in the street called her a slag) but really you should know better.'

Doctor: 'Ok, Ok, keep your hair on.'

SCENE TWO: The same doctor is in consultation room with pregnant 16-year-old Eve and her mother – Mrs Brown.

Doctor: 'Hello Eve, I see you've brought your mother with you. Hello eh Mrs eh Brown. Well Eve what are we going to do about you then you silly girl? What do you think Mrs Brown, what do you want her to do about it? She could have an abortion you know, it's not too late.'

SCENE THREE: Mrs Brown is talking to her sister.

Mrs Brown: 'I know, I wasn't upset last year when Denise got pregnant [pause and nodding of head]. I know Denise was only 17 but then Denise has got Dan and they are so settled; he's such a lovely lad and a good provider, but Eve, you know, she hasn't got a steady boyfriend.'

SCENE FOUR: [A while later] Eve is talking on the phone to a friend.

Eve: 'Well I know I didn't mean to get pregnant but I loved being pregnant and I was so looking forward to having a baby, I'd have worked really hard at being a good mum and when I lost her they all said "Well it's for the best isn't it?" But I don't think it is.'

The involvement of young women in these supporting materials was positively received by all professionals and practitioners who have attended the training so far. However, evaluation of the training has demonstrated that even more significant and 'powerful' was the involvement of young women in the actual training days. Young women participated in all of the training activities which at times training participants found 'embarrassing' or 'restricting', for example at the beginning of the first session when discussing the stereotypes surrounding teenage pregnancy and young parenthood. Yet, by the end of the first day, and reiterated through the verbal and written evaluation at the end of the training, the inclusion of young women as trainers was considered by most participants to be the most valuable part of the experience. Furthermore, involvement in the production and/or presentation of the training sometimes led to additional involvement in support agendas of the Teenage Pregnancy Strategy, including participation in the Young Parents' Forum and involvement in the Coventry Pals in Pregnancy programme, supporting other young women through their antenatal experience.

Young parents: specialist services

One year into the pilot provision of the specialist service, it was decided by Coventry TPPB that it was necessary to find a way to continue to resource this service. With this in mind, we were asked to put forward a proposal to undertake an evaluation of the service. This provided us with the opportunity to identify the extent to which such provision assists in breaking down the barriers that have traditionally characterized pregnant teenagers' and young parents' experience of ante- and postnatal services and, hopefully, to contribute to improving their health and well-being further.

In brief the aims and objectives of the evaluation were:

AIMS

1   To identify if current specialist services meet the needs of pregnant teenagers and young parents.
2   To identify how specialist services can be improved.

OBJECTIVES

1   To identify if current specialist services meet the needs of pregnant teenagers and young parents.
   a   To identify factors influencing pregnant teenagers and/or young parents' decisions to access services.
   b   To identify potential barriers pregnant teenagers and/or young parents may experience in accessing the services provided.
   c   To explore pregnant teenagers' and/or young parents' perception of the services provided.
   d   To identify what factors professionals view as influencing use of specialist services.

e   To identify what professionals view as potential barriers for take-up of
    specialist services.
f   To explore professionals' perception of the services provided.

2 To identify how specialist services can be improved.
   a   Identify areas of service provision pregnant teenagers and/or young
       parents view as positive and negative.
   b   Identify ways in which service users and professionals feel that service
       needs to be developed.

In order to achieve the aims and objectives of the evaluation we adopted
a multi-method qualitative approach to the research and undertook the
following:

- observation of the service;
- examination of the internal evaluations;
- single interviews and focus group interviews with 15 young mothers aged
  between 17 and 21 (five of whom accessed the service for one year or
  more) and six professionals: one midwife, two Connexions workers, two
  health visitors and one teenage pregnancy coordinator (which comprised
  the professional group supporting the specialist service at the time of
  the evaluation).

In our analysis we were concerned to identify key themes and address
the specific research questions outlined above whilst remaining open to the
possibility of unexpected findings. In analysing the data we looked for the
following:

- better support;
- partnership working;
- involving young parents;
- good and creative practice;
- sustainability.

The importance we attach to these issues is also reflected in policy documents and guides such as *National Service Framework for Children, Young People
and Maternity Services* (DoH 2004) and *Teenage Pregnancy: Who Cares? A Guide
to the Commissioning of Maternity Services* (Teenage Pregnancy Unit *et al.* 2004).
They are also suggested by the Health Development Agency as evaluative tools
to support the Teenage Pregnancy Strategy.

In our final report we presented our key findings in terms of 'Evidence of
Good Practice and Positive Experiences' and 'Problems and Challenges' and
concluded the report with the following recommendations:

- Secure new larger accommodation.
- Adhere to health and safety regulations, which will necessitate appropriate training for all participating professionals.
- Review session length and content.
- Establish clear lines of accountability for professionals and clear management support. This could involve the production of a briefing paper outlining the aims and objectives of the scheme and the involvement of each professional, which each professional participant and their manager signs. A paper such as this not only protects professionals but if revised annually has the added benefit of providing an ongoing history of the project that will be useful for further funding demands and for new professionals coming into the service. In addition the internal evaluation needs to be more comprehensive and rigorous (the research team were only able to access 11 completed evaluations in total) and feed more directly into developing the service.
- Consider further (professionals involved are already doing this) how to:
  - provide a service that meets ante- and postnatal needs;
  - encourage participants to 'move-on' to other services – perhaps the Young Parents' Forum or other 'mainstream' mothers and toddlers type groups;
  - provide a service that is attractive to and meets the needs of **all** young mothers and young fathers.

(Brown *et al.* 2005)

The findings and recommendations from the completed evaluation were presented to the sub-committee of the TPPB and to the TPPB itself. Since the presentation of our full report (Brown *et al.* 2005), Coventry TPPB have committed themselves to long-term funding of the specialist service (costs will eventually be mainstreamed within Coventry Primary Care Trust) and secured larger premises. Our other recommendations are currently under consideration.

Opportunities and barriers

As the above examples demonstrate, extending our involvement beyond traditionally defined research boundaries has enabled us to remain involved in positive policy developments at the local level (not just in Coventry but in the other districts/regions where we have undertaken 'Young Parent' projects). In addition to the impact on policy makers and practitioners, these projects are concerned with direct impact both on the respondents who took part in the studies and on the wider population of young people who were, or could become, either pregnant or parents. However, we remain frustrated that at present the impact of our challenge to negative representations remains negligible within national policy initiatives and lay discourses. Within the latest UK government policy initiatives on teenage pregnancy and young parenthood there is a recognition of support needs, however:

> ... for example, while the Supporting Families Green Paper offers many tempting morsels to those who would wish to see the development of some form of family policy, closer examination suggests that it has a strong social control agenda embedded within the rhetoric.
>
> (James and James 2001: 224)

As it stands the Teenage Pregnancy Strategy supports the view that the sexual activity in which young men and women engage is inappropriate and that this sexual 'promiscuity' automatically marks them as 'bad parents'. The, arguably impossible, target for prevention – [to] halve the under-18 conception rate in England by 2010 – has led to some TPPBs over-concentrating on prevention at the neglect of support. Further, the support agenda's focus on productivity outside the home, given the objective to 'increase the participation of teenage mothers in education, training or work to 60 per cent by 2010 to reduce the risk of long-term social exclusion' (SEU 1999 and see Chapter 5) negates the parental experience of young parents. With this in mind, at the end of a project focusing on the experience and support needs of 'young' fathers in Warwickshire (Letherby *et al.* 2004: 62), we wrote:

> The current emphasis on prevention first and foremost and support in relation to engaging in education and work both stigmatises pregnant teenagers, 'young' parents and 'young' families and ignores the significance of family life. Surely work with pregnant teenagers and with 'young' parents and families is all about support – supporting individuals and couples to make the right choices for them and supporting them to enact those choices.

However, despite the positive response from Warwickshire TPPB to this suggestion, and despite the impact of our work at a local level, and although we have been asked to represent this work at both regional and national events, the national priority remains the reduction of teenage pregnancy. The most recent statistics on conception seem to suggest that the strategy has had some success:

> The provisional 2004 under-18 conception rate for England is 41.5 per 1000 girls aged 15–17. This rate represents an overall decline of 11.1 per

cent since 1998 – the baseline year for the Teenage Pregnancy Strategy – and compares with a decline of 9.8 per cent between 1998 and 2003.

The provisional under-16 conception rate for England in 2004 is 7.5 per 1000 girls aged 13–15. This is 15.2 per cent lower than the Teenage Pregnancy Strategy's 1998 baseline rate of 8.8 conceptions per 1000 girls aged 13–15.

(National Statistics 2006)

However, there was also a notable increase between 1998 and 2004 in the percentage of conceptions that led to termination and the CSJ 'Pregnancy and Post-Natal Experience of Young Women who Become Pregnant under the Age of 20 Years' project (Letherby *et al.* 2002) and the more recent 'Support Prior to and Following Termination and Miscarriage for Young Women' project (Brady *et al.* 2006) suggest that the decisions that young women make are sometimes influenced by the views and desires of significant professional and familial others, reflecting their power and control in the situation of teenage pregnancy and parenthood (e.g. Letherby *et al.* 2002; Brown *et al.* 2006).

When research is commissioned locally and its findings reflect local agendas and priorities there is much more likelihood that researchers will be satisfied by the response of commissioners to their findings and will be involved and included in further policy and practice developments. Conversely, research – either commissioned or supported by funding councils – that challenges current practices is likely less to be positively received and enacted upon (see earlier discussion under 'What Works?').

End points

In this chapter, the last of four focusing on the process of putting our extending social research approach into practice, we have considered barriers to and opportunities for extending social research to the stage of implementation. The examples that we draw on provide empirical support for Fox's (2003) argument for 'practice-based research' or 'practically engaged research'. Thus, like Fox (2003: 87), we have found that the research can become 'part of the setting it is exploring and research becomes a facet of practice, inextricably tied up with the wider issues of political engagement, power and justice'. The three propositions of 'practice-based research' or 'practically engaged research' (Fox 2003: 90) are that:

The pursuit of knowledge must be recognized as a *local and contingent process* ... Secondly, research as a political activity should be *constitutive of difference* ... Thirdly, theory building ... should be seen not as an end in itself but as an *adjunct to practical activity* within the setting in question.

(Fox 2003: 87, author's emphasis)

It is not only in this chapter that we provide evidence of this in practice but throughout this section of the book (Chapters 5–8). Furthermore, it is not only in this section – but rather throughout the book – that our argument supports and develops further Fox's ideas.

Section 4

REFLECTIONS

9

Where are we now?

Paul Bywaters and Gayle Letherby

Introduction • Arguments and evidence • Research policy implications
• What have we learnt?

Introduction

As we stated at the outset, our aim in this book has been to bring together a
disparate literature about enhancing the impact of research in a new way; to
move the focus of attention in discussing impact from what happens after
research is completed to making it a central factor in the whole research process; and to illustrate and debate the implications of this shift through the
critical discussion of practice examples of mainly locally based research drawn
from our experience.

  We began with, and on occasion have returned to, a criticism of the social
research textbook genre, which (largely) unproblematically defines the end of
research as the final report and/or the publication of academic outputs. With
this in mind we do not claim to have solved the problem we identified by
writing an alternative text; rather we see this book as (in part) a critique of
existing social research texts (and courses). Having said that, we have outlined
our own epistemological views on and practical experiences of putting our
extending social research approach into practice and in this chapter we devote
a small amount of attention to issues of curricula. Perhaps then we have produced what Sue Wise and Liz Stanley (2003) call an opinionated text. Indeed,

we hope that it finds its way to undergraduate and postgraduate social research reading lists as a challenge and addition to what has gone before.

Another of our concerns and a motivating factor in the production of this book is the difference between the rhetoric and reality of the research funding and academic labour production agendas. At one and the same time social researchers are criticized for their lack of attention to and understanding of 'real world' issues and penalized if the number and 'quality' of their traditional research outputs falls. With this in mind this book is our contribution to the debate concerning current tensions and challenges for those who work in academia (see, for example, Morley and Walsh 1995; Trowler 1998; Howie and Tauchert 2001; Jary and Jones 2006).

In the rest of this final chapter, we re-evaluate some of the arguments and the evidence we have presented and draw together arguments about the relationship of our model to a number of aspects of research policy and practice. Finally we reflect on what we have learnt from the process of preparing and writing the book.

Arguments and evidence

A lynchpin of our argument has been that all social scientific research is about change. As we said in Chapter 4, all research is an intervention. Therefore, managing the impact that research has must be a responsibility of the researcher. We dealt with the question of whether knowledge in its own right could be the purpose of research in Chapter 2, but an account of the research process which suggests that managing the process makes the outcomes predictable would be extremely mechanical. In practice, you often cannot predict what the relevance of the findings of a given piece of research will be to a particular context. Not infrequently, it is the by-products of research that are more interesting than the intended focus. In particular, the *process* of carrying out research may have greater effects on the host organization than the formal findings. For example, the research process may force staff to reflect on what they do and why. It may bring together people with common interests across organizations who would not otherwise meet. It can point up limitations in information systems when information is sought for purposes not usually required. One of us – Paul Bywaters – was recently involved in an evaluation of a particular approach to social care after hospital discharge for a national voluntary organization. While the intended focus was on the adequacy of the level of financial support for these projects, important data was gleaned about the variability of record and management systems in different local projects and hence about the relationship between a national initiative and locally based organizations. So while we do think that the production of outputs and outcomes can be planned for, we are not wanting to suggest that the potential impact of research can be entirely programmed in advance, any more than the rest of the research process. This is further recognition, as outlined in Chapter 3, of the research process as 'messy' as opposed to 'hygienic'.

A second fundamental concern that we think some would raise is that our espousal of close working relationships between researchers and other stakeholders could result in inappropriate influences on the research process and findings (Chapter 8). Certainly, at times, the processes of negotiating and maintaining sometimes substantial sets of relationships with stakeholders who have different interests can be complex and time-consuming. But our experience is not on the whole that close relationships cause difficulties but rather that it is relationships that are distant or conflictual that lead to problems in ensuring that research is carried out as required or that findings result in action. Where relationships are conflictual, for example, because researchers and funders have different expectations about what is possible, it can be difficult to complete the research process effectively (see Chapter 7) and such conflict is likely to be reflected in funders' responses to findings, particularly where researchers have lost the trust of other stakeholders. Similarly, distant relationships between researchers and funders or other stakeholders are also likely to affect funders' sense of ownership of and interest in the results.

A third theoretical issue that we want to reconsider is the relationship between research and practice – or policy. Our examples are mainly of single studies and yet we are arguing for such studies to have a direct impact on service provision or policy making even though such evidence falls well below that often considered to be the highest standard: the meta-analysis or systematic review of randomized controlled trials (RCT). Of course, the cumulative evidence provided by a number of studies of the same or equivalent issues will usually be stronger than the single study. But such an approach can have the effect of designing out complexity with the consequence that the value of different kinds of study may be distorted. For example, randomized controlled trials are designed to test interventions where many characteristics of the individual respondent can be ignored because the size of the sample allows for positive or negative effects to be identified. Such an approach works quite effectively in the development of some medical and pharmaceutical treatments, although not without substantial drawbacks including the limitations of such an approach in being able to identify which individuals will and will not benefit. Paradoxically, by focusing on methods which seek to obscure the context in which interventions are made, findings are produced which can only predict benefits for populations, not for individual cases. Moreover, in most social interventions the complexity of the situation of the study makes RCTs either impossible or undesirable and meta-analyses risk obscuring important variables in the local context of constituent studies. While we clearly support the importance of research users having an appropriate critical stance to reading research, this does not mean that readers should not consider the relevance of single studies for the particular practice situations in which they were carried out or the possibility of their relevance in others.

The examples we have drawn on to explore our approach in practice are not representative of all social scientific research. Most of our examples are of:

- small projects, not major research programmes;
- local projects rather than national or international ones;
- projects funded by service providers or policy makers rather than research councils.

So, does this make a significant difference?

We do not believe that the kinds of evidence and experience we have drawn on change the underlying arguments about our approach. Whether projects are small and local or large and national or international, the issues involved in managing the process to maximize appropriate impact, to produce effectively targeted outputs or generate effective outcomes are equally relevant. The scale of the project clearly will affect the practice involved in extending social research, for example how to manage the publicity and politics of major and complex research projects, especially where there are popular or political interests at stake. It is no accident that many of our projects have been funded by service providers and policy makers as they are likely to have a more direct concern with the practical outcomes of their limited resources. But other funders, too, increasingly emphasize the importance of impact in their statements about the research they wish to fund. In addition, as highlighted earlier (see especially Chapter 2), we are not by any means the only social researchers concerned with these issues. Social scientists from our own and other disciplines, national and internationally are concerned with making research count and with thinking about new ways – beyond the traditionally defined researcher role – to ensure that this happens.

We would also criticize our research examples for insufficiently including accounts of work alongside service users and respondents. One of the key skills that researchers operating in an extended mode will have to learn is to negotiate the research process with a range of stakeholders who have sometimes overlapping but not identical interests. Our experience is that often service provider funders have only a limited understanding of what research can and cannot deliver; false expectations may be held by others too. In our experience, service providers may expect too much, for example, clear proof of the effectiveness of a particular intervention when the complexity of the situation, ethical considerations and lack of time and funding make such conclusions unavailable. On the other hand, service users and carers often have little or no expectations that research will produce concrete benefits and may be reluctant to engage for that reason. Their cynicism is not necessarily ill-founded. A recent examination of access to health services by black and minority ethnic communities, led by Paul Bywaters, involved community members at all stages and was well supported by the health service managers who had commissioned the research. But budget problems coupled with (yet another) reorganization of the health trust boundaries meant that there was only limited capacity to respond to the recommendations. While we have learnt to involve users routinely in projects we are undertaking, we have only rarely been partners in projects that are user-controlled, although we would support many of the values and arguments Michael Turner and Peter Beresford's (2005) report advances in contrasting user control with user participation.

Research policy implications

The extending social research approach, although in line with the many recommendations for research to be more relevant and usable and for policy and practice to be informed by evidence that we have referred to earlier, nevertheless exposes a series of policy issues, some for research funders and others for researchers. Here we highlight three significant issues:

- research training for extending social research;
- user involvement or user control in extending social research; and
- obstacles to extending social research in current funding policies.

A major challenge for researchers – and particularly for research training – is to reorient teaching towards the different and wider range of skills that are implied in our approach. Fundamentally, undergraduate and even postgraduate training and the textbooks on which they are based have focused on a limited range of methodological and ethical issues. Many research training courses still take a 'laboratory techniques' approach to the research process, training individuals in developing research questions and ethical concerns with informed consent, constructing questionnaires and using pre-set tests, the statistical analysis of data and the production of tables and charts, with relatively little opportunity for discussion of the many other aspects of the process. As we have argued earlier, they rarely discuss a set of 'real world' issues including:

- how to identify sources of funding;
- how to write a proposal for a funder;
- how to decide on ethical issues relating to sources of research funding;
- how to decide on ethical issues about user involvement;
- when and how to identify and approach prospective research partners;
- how to negotiate collaborative relationships with other stakeholders in developing a proposal;
- how to cost research proposals;
- when and how to set up, cost and work with steering groups;
- how to deal with emotions and relationships in the research process;
- how to develop recommendations from findings;

- how to identify research audiences;
- how to communicate effectively with a range of research audiences in writing, orally and in other ways;
- how to develop and maintain working relationships with a wide range of communication media.

There is an important need for those teaching research to re-examine current curricula and re-evaluate the required elements of research training.

This applies just as significantly at doctoral level. Although there has been some movement in the UK on the expectations stated by the ESRC of the required elements of research degree training, doctorates still largely stand or fall by the production of a thesis – a particular written form of reporting research which rarely discusses the application or implementation of findings and often does not even consider the relevance of findings to concrete social situations. In fact the dominance of the traditional form of thesis and its accompanying viva as the ordeal through which mature research status is achieved may be a significant factor in holding back the development of the wider range of skills required by paid researchers. Of course, the intensity of the doctoral process is valuable in developing significant research 'muscles' but it may result in researchers who are only partly 'fit for purpose' – able to debate finer points of methodology but unable to cost a research proposal or know how to write a press release to publicize the findings.

In addition, opportunities for undergraduates and masters students to learn by doing, to undertake real research even on a small scale are being reduced. The development of research governance systems and data protection laws already means that in most UK universities there are few opportunities for students of health professions to undertake empirical research even with health service staff, never mind patients, at undergraduate or even masters levels. This is liable to extend to other professional training programmes, such as social work degrees, as social care research becomes subject to the same governance arrangements as the health care system (Working Group on Ethical Review of Student Research in the NHS (Doyal Committee) 2005). Research access consent processes have become too time-consuming, often requiring approvals from university research ethics committees, local research ethics committees, from NHS trust research committees and from line managers of relevant departments before potential individual respondents are asked whether or not they are willing to participate. The timescales required to secure consent preclude the possibility of undergraduate projects being completed in the usual timescales and the volume and training focus of the projects (coupled with the novice status of the students) will often make them unsuccessful and leave the student without an alternative.

The presumption in current thinking about research governance tends towards emphasizing risk rather than competence. A working party on student research projects in health and social care went out of its way to emphasize the risks involved:

. . . effective assessment of any risk or inconvenience to which participants may be exposed is also of the utmost importance. For example, when undergraduate students interview patients, they risk causing distress and thus potential complications in the patient's illness or recovery. The fact that such harm may be rare does not obviate the moral importance of avoiding it.

(Working Group on Ethical Review of Student Research
in the NHS 2005: 6)

The increase in the numbers of students on many research modules due to both external drivers for 'mass' higher education and internal drivers for so-called 'modular efficiency' (Jary and Jones 2006) does make close supervision of student projects difficult. The cautious approach also means that adults (patients or service users) are usually no longer assumed to be able to give their own consent to participate without projects first being screened by institutional structures even in research that is highly unlikely to have any personal consequences, perhaps as much because of fears of possible legal action as because of concerns about protecting individual respondents. The consequences of this growing caution about research is potentially very significant for the research literacy of subsequent generations of professionals or of other students. While the Doyal Committee recommended the establishment of supplementary Student Project Ethics Committees, many universities and local trusts have concluded that empirical undergraduate student projects cannot be managed in any of the practice-based disciplines (for example, health, social care, education). Yet, it is these disciplines which face particular problems in developing a research-informed workforce and in training skilled researchers (ESRC 2006c). The training implications of current governance and data protection policies need to be reconsidered as well as the wider impact on what kinds of research are undertaken and by whom.

In contrast to this protective approach by gatekeepers of access to research (admittedly following the discovery of widespread experimentation without consent, for example, involving the bodies of dead babies (Royal Liverpool Children's Inquiry 2000)), there is increasing institutional support within health research in particular for 'patient' or lay participation in research processes through a variety of mechanisms. In several respects the struggle for user participation and the principles of user-controlled research echo our arguments for extending our research models. The risk in user involvement is that a small number of lay participants will become absorbed by the existing and powerful research interests rather than creating a genuine opening up of research to a wider range of influences or to control by other than professional researchers. As Michael Turner and Peter Beresford put it (2005: 6): 'User involvement in research tends to be compared unfavourably with user-controlled research because the former is seen to embody inequalities of power which work to the disadvantage of service users.' There are profound conflicts here between powerful interests. The current UK Department of Health policy has come a long way in now advocating that users should usually be involved in research management processes, but the degree of power allowed is the contentious issue. The relevance of this to our argument is the perception – from service users at least – that user-controlled research is more likely to produce change than 'academic' research. As one respondent in the 'Involve' project on user-controlled research phrased it: 'I would like to see user research used more effectively because academics do a lot of research and it just ends up on the shelf. I'd like to see research used and shared for it to become the driver behind service delivery' (Turner and Beresford (2005: 82). Turner and Beresford concluded: 'Both the literature review and the service users who took part in this project prioritised *making change* as a key purpose of user-controlled research (2005: 89).'

As well as users' emphasis on change, funders are also increasingly emphasizing their commitment to research that makes an impact. For example, in the UK, the new ESRC Impact Grants funding stream is designed to provide additional funds to help researchers develop the impact and application of their work (ESRC 2006d). So there is the basis for common cause with researchers who are interested in the extending social research model. However, a further obstacle exists in the UK in the way in which research careers are shaped by research funding policies. The largest explicit research funding stream for UK universities comes from the Higher Education Funding Councils and is based on the results of successive 'Research Assessment Exercises' (see www.rae.ac.uk). The measures of research excellence used place very little emphasis on the impact of findings or on the processes which would ensure that findings were made widely available and accessible. In many subjects journal articles are weighted according to so-called 'impact factors' that reflect not impact on the external world but the extent to which papers are cited by other writers, usually academics. The panels which assess the quality of the research submitted are also largely made up of academics rather than either end users or the wider public who might be expected to benefit from research. There is recognition for how much funding has been brought in, but that gained from research councils tends to be weighted more highly than that from service providers or charities. Measures of research 'esteem' may include marks of public recognition, media coverage, awards from industry and so on, but count for less than 10 per cent of the final research quality score.

As we argued in Chapter 2 and have reiterated elsewhere in the book, such 'scores' in the RAE are, for most UK university-based researchers, the single most public mark of recognition and have a dominating influence on departmental research policies, including systems of reward and promotion, and career advancement by moves to other institutions are also often based upon the potential of the appointee to bring RAE success. Researchers are encouraged by this policy framework to focus their time on publishing in a narrow range of elite journals and in securing funding from sources which weigh theoretical and methodological excellence more highly than excellence in securing the application and implementation of results. The processes of relationship building and maintenance with a wide range of stakeholders, of devoting time to making findings widely available and understood and helping to translate findings into outcomes will receive relatively little reward. As a result researchers are likely to be faced with difficult dilemmas about the use of their time.

It is clear that there are significant levers available to force researchers to extend the range of their research practice. If funders weighted much more highly the plans for outputs and outcomes in the judgements they made about who received funding, the message would rapidly produce behavioural change. If measures of research quality paid much greater attention to the ways in which researchers had used the evidence they gained and these were linked to research funding, practice would fall into line. After all, most researchers would also like to see their work making a difference.

A final policy consideration in the UK is a complex funding policy recently introduced, which requires universities to charge for their research activity in particular ways or to face financial penalties – the so-called 'full economic cost' regime (HEFCE 2006). Based on a belief that funding for teaching was being used to subsidize research activity in universities, the UK government required a particular formula for research costing which requires charging high levels of 'overheads' on top of researchers' salaries and other marginal costs such as those for transport, subsistence or transcribing. Even the national research councils, essentially government quangos, are not usually paying the 'full economic cost', while the effect has been to price universities out of the market of much research funded by commercial, public sector or charitable organizations where they are often competing with private sector research companies. The unanticipated side effect of this central policy change is to reduce the research which universities undertake directly for partners who are most likely to be interested in research that produces change.

What have we learnt?

This has been a personal book in the sense that it has arisen out of our personal experience of carrying out mainly funded research for a variety of funders, particularly organizations providing social care, health or other services. It is personal in that it reflects our experiences and interests as a sociologist (Letherby) and a social work academic (Bywaters) with the overlapping but different perspectives that this brings to our work.

Our experience of working with (and sometimes clearly at cross purposes with) our research funders and other stakeholders is that there are multiple concerns that have a considerable impact on the value of the research but are rarely discussed by methodologists and/or taught to new researchers. This, perhaps, explains why we have frequently encountered the suspicion amongst funders and commissioners who do not know us that we will be academics who have little understanding of their realities (although we also appreciate that other influences, for example some media representations of academics and the academic job, might also be at play here). Our experience of services users and respondents who have been researched before is that they are also often sceptical about the potential of research to make an impact, about the relevance of academic research to their concerns and about the commitment of the researchers' involvement beyond the production of the 'final' report. Our experience of research assistants, often people with good qualifications up to and including doctorates, is that they often have little knowledge of the nuts and bolts of funded research, including such basic aspects as how to approach the task of getting funded, how to work with funders and others throughout and beyond the traditionally defined research process and how to publicize findings beyond the academy. If they do have experience of these things, it will not have been gained during their formal research training. Those we have worked with have shared our interest in bringing about change, but that has not been their previous experience of research. These people cannot all be wrong – their desire for a more applied approach to research deserves listening to.

What has inspired us as social scientists is the impact which the study of society can have on human lives. Both of us are admirers of Charles Wright Mills's *The Sociological Imagination* (1959) and we have been impressed also by the recent debates concerning the public and political aspects of social science (see Chapter 2), which remind us of the significance of Mills's work to understanding the social world of today. As Liz Stanley (2005: 5.4) notes:

> There is a further dimension of the sociological imagination relevant here. For Mills, sociologists like other people can best understand themselves, their lives and those of others by locating themselves within the times (on which, see also Gouldner 1970), and he specifically sees the sociological imagination as rooted in and growing out of this (Mills 1959: 5–6). Relatedly, Mills also writes about the 'kinds of effort that lie behind the development of the sociological imagination' and its 'implications for political as well as for cultural life' (Mills 1959: 18).

Mills closed this classic text by arguing that through relating 'the human meaning of public issues' to the private troubles of the individual life 'the sociological imagination has its chance to make a difference in the quality of human life in our time' (248). In the end this is the nub of our whole argument and although we are no longer the 'young social scientists' that David Silverman (1999: 273) feels will soon be disabused of their desire to make a difference, we still hope that we can. For us the point of social science is to produce or support change and to promote social justice. For this, current and subsequent generations of social science researchers will need all the intellectual skill, honesty and engagement available.

References

Abbott, P., Wallace, C. and Tyler, M. (2005) *Introduction to Sociology: Feminist Perspectives*. London: Routledge.

Alkin, M. (1985) *A Guide for Evaluation Decision Makers*. Beverley Hills, CA: Sage Publications.

Allender, P. and Quigley, A. (2005) *Challenging Hate Crime in Coventry: Research Report*. Coventry: Centre for Social Justice, Coventry University and Coventry Community Safety Partnership.

Alvesson, M. (2002) *Postmodernism and Social Research*. Buckingham: Open University Press.

Arai, L. (2003) British policy on teenage pregnancy and childbearing: the limitations of comparisons with other European countries, *Critical Social Policy*, 23(1): 89–102.

Argote, L. and Ingram, P. (2000) Knowledge transfer: a basis for competitive advantage in firms, *Organizational Behaviour and Human Decision Processes*, 82(1): 150–69.

Australian Research Council (2005) *Who Are We?* Canberra: Australian Research Council, www.arc.gov.au/about_arc/default.htm. Accessed November 2005.

Barnes, C. and Mercer, G. (1997) Breaking the mould: an introduction to doing disability research, in C. Barnes and G. Mercer (eds) *Doing Disability Research*. Leeds: The Disability Press.

Bauman, Z. (1990) *Thinking Sociologically*. Oxford: Blackwell.

Becker, H. (1967) Whose side are we on?, *Social Problems*, 14: 239–47.

Beresford, P. (2000) Service users' knowledges and social work theory: conflict or collaboration?, *British Journal of Social Work*, 30: 489–503.

Beresford, P. (2002) User involvement in research and evaluation: liberation or regulation?, *Social Policy and Society*, 1: 95–105.

Beresford, P. (2003) User involvement in research: exploring the challenges, *NT Research* 8(1): 36–46.

Beresford, P. and Evans, C. (1999) Research note: research and empowerment, *British Journal of Social Work*, 29(5): 671–8.

Blackmore, J. and Lauder, H. (2005) Researching policy, in B. Somekh and C. Lewin (eds) *Research Methods in the Social Sciences*. London: Sage Publications.

Blaxter, M., Hughes, C. and Tight, M. (2001) *How to Research*. Buckingham: Open University Press.

Bloor, M. (1999) Addressing social problems through qualitative research, in D. Silverman (ed.) *Qualitative Research: Theory, Method and Practice*. London: Sage Publications.

Blunkett, D. (2000) 'Influence or irrelevance: can social science improve government?' Secretary of State's ESRC Lecture Speech, *2 February*. London: Department for Education and Employment.

Bowling, A. (2002) *Research Methods in Health*, 2nd edn. Buckingham: Open University Press.

Brady, G., Brown, G. and Letherby, G. (2005) *Entry/Exit/Post-Exit Consultation Strategy for Pregnant Teenagers and Young Parents Accessing Supported Housing in Coventry: 'Good Practice Guide'*. Coventry: Centre for Social Justice, Coventry University.

Brady, G., Brown, G., Letherby, G., Bayley, J. and Wallace, L. (2006) *Support Prior to and Following Termination and Miscarriage for Pregnant Teenagers and Young Parents in Coventry*. Coventry: Centre for Social Justice and Health Services Research Centre, Coventry University.

Braye, S. (2000) Participation and involvement in social care: an overview, in H. Kemshall and R. Littlechild (eds) *User Involvement and Participation in Social Care*. London: Jessica Kingsley.

Broughton, T. (1994) Life lines: writing and writer's block in the context of women's studies, in S. Davies, C. Lubelska and J. Quinn (eds) *Changing the Subject: Women in Higher Education*. London: Taylor and Francis.

Brown, G., Brady, G. and Letherby, G. (2005) *An Evaluation of Specialist Services for Pregnant Teenagers and Young Parents*. Coventry: Centre for Social Justice, Coventry University.

Brown, G., Brady, G. and Letherby, G. (2006) *Power and Control in the Intimate and Personal Relationships of Pregnant Teenagers and Young Mothers*. Coventry: Centre for Social Justice, Coventry University.

BSA (British Sociological Association) (2002) *Statement of Ethical Practice for the British Sociological Association*, www.britsoc.co.uk/user_doc/Statement%20of%20Ethical%20Practice.doc. Accessed May 2006.

Bulmer, M. (ed.) (1987) *Social Science Research and Government: Comparative Essays on Britain and the United States*. Cambridge: Cambridge University Press.

Bunting, L. and McAuley, C. (2004) Research review: teenage pregnancy and motherhood: the contribution of support, *Child and Family Social Work*, 9(2): 207–16.

Burawoy, M. (2005) For public sociology, *American Sociological Review*, 70: 4–28.

Butler, I. (2002) Critical commentary (a code of ethics for social work research), *British Journal of Social Work*, 32(2): 239–48.

Butt, J. and O'Neil, A. (2004) *'Let's Move On': Black and Minority Ethnic Older People's Views on Research Findings*. York: Joseph Rowntree Foundation.

Bywaters, P. and Rolfe, A. (2002) *Look Beyond The Scars*. London: NCH.

Cabinet Office (1999) *Modernising Government*. London: The Stationery Office.

Canadian Social Science and Humanities Research Council (2005) *Knowledge Impact on Society. An SSHRC Transformation Program*, www.sshrc.ca/web/apply/program_descriptions/knowledge_impact_e.asp. Accessed June 2006.

Cannon, L. W., Higgenbotham, E. and Leung, M. L. A. (1991) Race and class bias in qualitative research on women, in M. M. Fonow and J. A. Cook (eds) *Beyond Methodology: Feminist Scholarship as Lived Experience*. Bloomington, IN: Indiana University Press.

Caplan, N. (1979) The two-communities theory and knowledge utilization, *American Behavioural Science*, 22(3): 459–70.

Carroll, D., Greenwood, R., Lynch, K., Sullivan, J., Ready, C. and Fitzmaurice, J. (1997) Barriers and facilitators to the utilization of nursing research, *Clinical Nurse Specialist*, 11(5): 207–12.

Cheek, J. (2000) An untold story: doing unfunded qualitative research, in N. Denzin and Y. Lincoln (eds) *The Handbook of Qualitative Research*, 2nd edn. Thousand Oaks, London, New Dehli: Sage Publications.

Coghlan, A. and du Boulay, D. (2004) *Addressing the challenge of institutional racism in a national charity: using a social justice approach.* Paper presented at the International Conference on Diversity, Los Angeles, July.

Collins, P. (1998) Negotiated selves: reflections on 'unstructured' interviewing, *Sociological Research Online* 3(3): www.socresonline.org.uk/socresonline/3/3/2.html.

Colombo, A. (forthcoming) Models of mental disorder: how philosophy and the social sciences can illuminate psychiatric ethics, in G. Widdershoven, T. Hope, L. Van Der Scheer and J. McMillan (eds) *Empirical Ethics in Psychiatry.* Oxford: Oxford University Press.

Colombo, A., Bendelow, G., Fulford, K. W. M. and Williams, S. (2003) Models of mental disorder: their influence on shared decision making in community mental health teams, *Social Science and Medicine*, 56: 1557–70.

Colombo, A., Fulford, K. W. M., Bendelow, G. and Williams, S. (2004) Model behaviour, *OpenMind*, Jan–Feb: 10–12.

Colombo, A. and Neary, M. (1998) 'Square roots and algebra': perceptions of risk/needs assessment measures in probation practice, *Probation Journal*, 45(4): 213–19.

Cook, J., Warren, L. and Maltby, T. (2003) *Older Women's Lives and Voices: Participation and Policy in Sheffield.* Sheffield: Economic and Social Research Council Growing Older Programme, Findings 21, University of Sheffield, www.shef.ac.uk/uni/projects/gop. Accessed June 2004.

Cook, J. A. and Fonow, M. M. (1980) Knowledge and women's interests: issues of epistemology and methodology in feminist sociological research, in J. McCarl Nielsen (ed.) *Feminist Research Methods: Exemplary Readings in the Social Sciences.* Boulder, CO: Westview.

Cormie, J. and Warren, L. (2001) *Working with Older People: Guidelines for Running Discussion Groups and Influencing Practice.* Bristol: The Policy Press.

Cotterill, P. (1992) Interviewing women: issues of friendship, vulnerability and power, *Women's Studies International Forum*, 15(5/6): 593–606.

Cotterill, P. and Letherby, G. (1993) Weaving stories: personal auto/biographies in feminist research, *Sociology*, 27(1): 67–80.

Cotterill, P. and Letherby, G. (1994) The person in the researcher, in R. Burgess (ed.) *Studies in Qualitative Methodology, Volume 4.* London: JAI Press.

Coventry TPPB (Teenage Pregnancy Partnership Board) (2002) *Teenage Pregnancy Strategy.* Coventry: Coventry Primary Care Trust.

Curtis, P. (2005) Lecturers' leader calls for end of research assessment, *Guardian Unlimited*, 21 April, http://education.guardian.co.uk/RAE/story/0,,1465034,00.html. Accessed June 2006.

Darlington, Y. and Scott, D. (2002) *Qualitative Research in Practice: Stories From The Field.* Buckingham: Open University Press.

David, M. (2002) Introduction: themed section on evidence-based policy as a concept for modernising governance and social science research, *Social Policy and Society*, 1(3): 213–14.

Davies, B. (forthcoming) Women and transgression in the halls of academe in *Studies in Higher Education.*

Davies, H., Nutley, S. and Smith, P. (2000) *What Works? Evidence-based Policy and Practice in Public Services.* Bristol: The Policy Press.

Davies, H., Nutley, S. and Walter, I. (2005) *Assessing the Impact of Social Science Research: Conceptual, Methodological and Practical Issues.* St. Andrews: Research Unit for Research Utilization.

Davis, A. (1992) Who needs user research? Service users as research subjects or participants; implications for user involvement in service contracting, in M. Barnes and G. Wistow (eds) *Researching User Involvement*. Leeds: Nuffield Institute for Health Services, University of Leeds.

Denscombe, M. (2002) *Ground Rules for Good Research*. Buckingham: Open University Press.

Denscombe, M. (2003) *The Good Research Guide*. Buckingham: Open University Press.

Denzin, N. K. and Lincoln, Y. S. (eds) (2003a) *Strategies of Qualitative Inquiry*. Thousand Oaks, CA: Sage Publications.

Denzin, N. K. and Lincoln, Y. S. (eds) (2003b) *Collecting and Interpreting Qualitative Materials*. Thousand Oaks, CA: Sage Publications.

DFEE (Department for Education and Employment) (1997) *Report of the National Committee of Inquiry into Higher Education* (Dearing Report). London: Department for Education and Employment.

DHSS (Department of Health and Social Security) (1980) *Inequalities in Health: Report of a Research Working Group*. London: Department of Health and Social Security.

DHSS (1991) *Local Research Ethics Committees*. London: Department of Health and Social Security.

Dickson, D. (2001) Weaving a social web, *Nature*, 414: 587.

Di-Stephano, C. (1990) Dilemmas of difference: feminism, modernity and postmodernism, in L. Nicholson (ed.) *Feminism/Postmodernism*. London: Routledge.

DoH (Department of Health) (1993) *Changing Childbirth. Report of the Expert Maternity Group* (Cumberlege Report). London: HMSO.

DoH (2001) *Governance Arrangements for NHS Research Ethics Committees*. London: Department of Health.

DoH (2002) *Government Response to the First Annual Report of the Independent Advisory Group on Teenage Pregnancy*. London: Department of Health.

DoH (2004) *National Service Framework for Children, Young People and Maternity Services: Executive Summary*. London: Department of Health.

DoH (2005) *Research Governance Framework for Health and Social Care*, 2nd edn. London: Department of Health.

DoH (2006) *Reward and Recognition: The Principles and Practice of Service User Payment and Reimbursement in Health and Social Care. A Guide for Service Providers, Service Users and Carers*. London: Department of Health.

DoH and Kings College London (2006) *Proceedings of a National Seminar on Social Care Research Capacity*. London: Social Care Workforce Research Unit, Kings College London.

Easterby-Smith, M., Thorpe, R. and Lowe, A. (1993) *Management Research: An Introduction*. London: Sage Publications.

Edwards, A. and Talbot, R. (1994) *The Hard-pressed Researcher*. London: Longman.

Effendi, K. and Hamber, B. (1999) Publish or perish: disseminating your research findings, in M. Terre Blanche and K. Durrheim (eds) *Research In Practice*. Cape Town: University of Cape Town Press.

Eliasson, G. (1996) *Firm Objectives, Controls and Organization: The Use of Information and the Transfer of Knowledge*. Dordrecht: Kluwer Academic Publishers.

Ellis, K. and Rummery, K. (2000) Politics into practice: the production of a disabled person's guide to accessing community care assessments, in H. Kemshall and R. Littlechild (eds) *User Involvement and Participation in Social Care: Research Informing Practice*. London: Jessica Kingsley.

Epstein, D. (1995) In our (new) right minds: the hidden curriculum and the academy, in L. Morley and V. Walsh (eds) *Feminist Academics: Creative Agents for Change*. London: Taylor and Francis.

ESRC (Economic and Social Research Council) (2001) *Developing a Media Strategy*, www.esrcsocietytoday.ac.uk/ESRCInfoCentre/Images/Media_tcm6–7381.pdf. Accessed August 2005.

ESRC (2005a) *Postgraduate Training Guidelines*, Section D, page 3, www.esrcsocietytoday. ac.uk/ESRCInfoCentre/Images/Section_D_General_Research_Skills_and_Transferable_ Skills_tcm6–9070.pdf. Accessed June 2006.

ESRC (2005b) *Building a Strong and Sustainable Future*, www.esrcsocietytoday.ac.uk/ ESRCInfoCentre/about/delivery%5Fplan/. Accessed May 2005.

ESRC (2005c) *General Guidance Notes on Constructing a Good Application, Part II*, www. esrcsocietytoday.ac.uk/ESRCInfoCentre/Support/research_award_holders/FAQs2/ index2.aspx. Accessed August 2005.

ESRC (2005d) *Grant Application Downloadable Academic Referee Reply Form*, ftp://ftp. esrc.ac.uk/Pub/AcadRefGrant.doc. Accessed August 2005.

ESRC (2006a) *Communications Toolkit*, www.esrcsocietytoday.ac.uk/ESRCInfoCentre/ Support/Communications%5FToolkit/. Accessed May 2006.

ESRC (2006b) *10 Top Tips in Media Relations*, www.esrcsocietytoday.ac.uk/ ESRCInfoCentre/Support/Communications_Toolkit/media_relations/top_ten_tips/ index.aspx. Accessed February 2006.

ESRC (2006c) *Demographic Review of the UK Social Sciences*, www.esrcsocietytoday.ac.uk/ ESRCInfoCentre/Images/Demographic_Review_tcm6–13872.pdf. Accessed June 2006.

ESRC (2006d) *Impact Grants*, www.esrc.ac.uk/impactgrants. Accessed June 2006.

Finch, J. (1984) It's great to have someone to talk to': the ethics and politics of interviewing women, in C. Bell and H. Roberts (eds) *Social Researching: Politics, Problems, Practice*. London: Routledge and Kegan Paul.

Fine, M. (1994) Dis-tance and other stances: negotiations of power inside feminist research, in A. Gitlin (ed.) *Power and Method: Political Activism and Educational Research*. London: Routledge.

Flax, J. (1987) Postmodernism and gender relations in feminist theory, *Signs: Journal of Women in Culture and Society*, 12: 334–51.

Ford, L. (2006) Group to develop new research funding model, *Guardian Unlimited*, 23 March, www.education.guardian.co.uk/RAE/story/0,,1738113,00.html. Accessed June 2006.

Fox, N. J. (2003) Practice-based evidence: towards collaborative and transgressive research, *Sociology*, 37(1): 81–102.

Frampton, C., Kinsman, G., Thompson, A. K. and Tilleczek, K. (2006) Social movement/ social research: towards political activist ethnography, in C. Frampton, G. Kinsman, A.K. Thompson and K. Tilleczek (eds) *Sociology for Changing the World: Social Movements/Social Research*. Novia Scotia: Fernwood.

French, B. (2005) Evaluating research for use in practice: what criteria do specialist nurses use?, *Journal of Advanced Nursing*, 50(3): 235–43.

Fulford, K.W.M. and Colombo, A. (2004) Six models of mental disorder: combining philosophic-analytic and empirical methods in a new research paradigm, *International Journal of Philosophy, Psychiatry and Psychology*, 35: 125–40.

Fulop, N. (2001) *Communication Strategy for the SDO Programme*. London: Department of Health.

Gaber, I. (2001) *Television and Radio: A Good Practice Guide*. Swindon: ESRC.

Genn, H. (2004) Judgements of quality in grant applications. Paper presented at ESRC Research Methods Festival, 1–3 July, St Catherine's College, Oxford.

Gibbs, L. and Gambill, E. (2002) Evidence based practice: counterarguments to objections, *Research on Social Work Practice*, 12(3): 452–76.

Giddens, A. (1985) *The Nation State and Violence*. Cambridge: Polity Press.

Giddens, A. (1999) *The Consequences of Modernity*. London: Polity Press.

Gilbert, N. (1993) *Researching Social Life*. Newbury Park, CA: Sage Publications.

Glucksmann, M. (1994) The work of knowledge and the knowledge of women's work, in M. Maynard and J. Purvis (eds) *Researching Women's Lives from a Feminist Perspective*. London: Taylor and Francis.

Gomm, R. (2004) *Social Research Methodology*. Basingstoke: Palgrave.

Gray, D. E. (2004) *Doing Research in the Real World*. London: Sage Publications.

Grayson, L. and Gomersall, A. (2003) *A Difficult Business: Finding the Evidence for Social Science Reviews*. London: ESRC UK Centre for Evidence Based Policy and Practice, Queen Mary College, University of London.

Grinyer, A. (1999) Anticipating the problem of contract social research, *Social Research Update*, Winter (27), www.soc.surrey.ac.uk/sru/SRU27.html.

Gubrium, J. F. and Wallace, J. B. (1990) Who theorises age?, *Ageing and Society*, 10(2): 131–49.

Hallowell, N., Lawton, J. and Gregory, S. (2005) *Reflections on Research*. Buckingham: Open University Press.

Hammersley, M. and Gomm, R. (1997) Bias in social research, *Sociological Research Online* 2(1), www.socresonling.org.uk/socresonline/2/4/7.html.

Harden, J., Scott, S., Brackett-Milburn, K. and Jackson, S. (2000) Can't talk, won't talk? Methodological issues in researching children, *Sociological Research Online*, 5(2), www.socresonline.org.uk/5/2.

Harding, S. (ed.) (1987) *Feminism and Methodology*. Milton Keynes: Open University Press.

Harding, S. (1993) Rethinking standpoint epistemology: 'what is strong objectivity?', in L. Alcoff and E. Porter (eds) *Feminist Epistemologies*. New York: Routledge.

Hart, E. and Bond, M. (1995) *Action Research for Health and Social Care: A Guide to Practice*. Buckingham: Open University Press.

Hart, S. (1997) Zero tolerance, in M. Ang-lygate, C. Corrin and H. Millsom (eds) *Desperately Seeking Sisterhood*. London: Taylor and Francis.

HEFCE (Higher Education Funding Council for England) (2004) *RAE Initial Decisions by the UK Funding Bodies*. Bristol: HEFCE.

HEFCE (2006) *Transparency Review*. Bristol: HEFCE, www.hefce.ac.uk/finance/fundinghe/TransparencyReview/. Accessed June 2006.

Henn, M., Weinstein, M. and Foard, N. (2005) *A Short Introduction to Social Research*. London: Sage Publications.

Hill Collins, P. (1989) Black feminist thought, *Signs: Journal of Women in Culture and Society*, 14(4): 745–73.

HM Treasury (2003) *Lambert Review of Business–University Collaboration*. London: Her Majesty's Stationery Office.

HM Treasury (2004) *Science and Innovation Investment Strategy 2004–2014*. Norwich: HMSO.

Hood, S., Mayall, B. and Oliver, S. (eds) (1999) *Critical Issues in Social Research*. Buckingham: Open University Press.

Howard, J. (2005) *The Emerging Business of Knowledge Transfer*. Sydney: Department of Education, Science and Training, Australian Government.

Howie, G. and Tauchert, A. (eds) (2001) *Gender, Teaching and Research in Higher Education: Challenges for the 21st Century*. London: Ashgate.

Huberman, M. (1987) Steps towards an integrated model of research utilization, *Knowledge*, June: 586–611.

Huberman, M. (1994) Research utilization: the state of the art, *Knowledge and Policy: International Journal of Knowledge Transfer and Utilization*, 74(4): 13–33.

Hughes, C. (ed.) (2003a) *Disseminating Qualitative Research in Educational Settings*. Maidenhead: Open University Press/McGraw-Hill.

Hughes, C. (2003b) Developing informed practice for disseminating qualitative research, in Christina Hughes (ed.) (2003) *Disseminating Qualitative Research in Educational Settings*. Buckingham: Open University Press.

Humphries, B. (1997) From critical thought to emancipatory action: contradictory research goals?, *Sociological Research Online*, 2(1), www.socresonline.org.uk/ socresonline/ 2/1/3.html.

Humphries, B. (1998) The baby and the bath water: Hammersley, Cealey Harrison and Hood-Williams and the emancipatory research debate, *Sociological Research Online* 3(1), www.socresonline.org.uk/socresonline/3/1/9.

Humphries, B. (ed.) (2000a) *Research in Social Care and Social Welfare: Issues and Debates for Practice*. London: Jessica Kingsley.

Iles, T. (ed.) (1992) *All Sides of the Subject: Women and Biography*. New York: Teachers College Press.

Innvaer, S., Vist, G., Trommald, M. and Oxman, A. (2002) Health policy-makers' perceptions of their use of evidence and systematic review, *Journal of Health Services Research and Policy*, 7(4): 239–44.

James, A. L. and James, A. (2001) Tightening the net: children, community and control, *British Journal of Sociology*, 52(2): 211–28.

Jary, D. and Jones, R. (eds) (2006) *Widening Participation in Higher Education – Issues, Research and Resources for the Social Sciences and Beyond*. Birmingham: C-SAP.

Jones, R.J.E. and Santaguida, P. (2005) Evidence-based practice and health policy development: the link between knowledge and action, *Physiotherapy*, 91(1): 14–21.

JRF (Joseph Rowntree Foundation) (2006) *Background to our Research and Development Work*, www.jrf.org.uk/funding/research/overview/background.asp. Accessed February 2006.

Katz-Rothman, B. (1996) Bearing witness: representing women's experiences of prenatal diagnosis, in S. Wilkinson and C. Kitzinger (eds) *Representing the Other: A Feminism and Psychology Reader*. London: Sage Publications.

Kelly, L., Burton, S. and Regan, L. (1994) Researching women's lives or studying women's oppression? Reflections on what constitutes feminist research, in M. Maynard and J. Purvis (eds) *Researching Women's Lives From a Feminist Perspective*. London: Taylor and Francis.

Ladwig, J. (1994) For whom this reform? Outlining educational policy as a social field, *British Journal of Sociology of Education*, 15(3): 341–63.

Landry, R., Amara, N. and Laamary, M. (1998) *Utilization of Social Science Research Knowledge in Canada*. Quebec, Canada: Department de Science Politique, Université Laval.

Lavis, J. N., Robertson, D., Woodside, J. M., McLeod, C. B., Abelson, J. and the Knowledge Transfer Study Group (2003) How can research organizations more effectively transfer research knowledge to decision makers?, *The Millbank Quarterly*, 81(2): 221–48.

Lee-Treweek, G. and Linkogle, S. (eds) (2000) *Danger in the Field: Risk and Ethics in Social Research*. London: Routledge.

Letherby, G. (2002) Claims and disclaimers: knowledge, reflexivity and representation in feminist research, *Sociological Research Online*, 6(4), www.socresonline.org.uk/6/4/letherby.html.

Letherby, G. (2003a) *Feminist Research in Theory and Practice*. Buckingham: Open University Press.

Letherby, G. (2003b) Reflections on where we are and where we want to be: response to 'Looking back and looking forward: some recent feminist sociology reviewed', *Sociological Research Online*, 8(4), www.socresonline.org.uk/8/4/letherby.html.

Letherby, G. (2004) Quoting and counting: an autobiographical response to Oakley, *Sociology*, 38(1): 175–89.

Letherby, G., Brady, G. and Brown, G. (2004) *Experience and Support Needs of 'Young' Fathers in Warwickshire*. Coventry: Centre for Social Justice, Coventry University.

Letherby, G., Brown, G. and Butler, C. (2003) *Housing Needs of Young Parents in Warwickshire*. Coventry: Centre for Social Justice, Coventry University.

Letherby, G., Brown, G., DiMarco, H. and Wilson, C. (2002) *Pregnancy and Post-Natal Experience of Young Women who Become Pregnant under the Age of 20 Years*. Coventry: Centre for Social Justice, Coventry University.

Letherby, G., Wilson, C., Bailey, N. and Brown, G. (2001) *Supported Semi-Independent Housing for Under-18 Lone Parents: Needs Assessment*. Coventry: Centre for Social Justice, Coventry University.

Letherby, G. and Zdrodowski, D. (1995) Dear researcher: the use of correspondence as a method within feminist qualitative research, *Gender and Society*, 9(5): 576–93.

Lewis, J. (2001) What works in community care?, *Managing Community Care*, 9(1): 3–6.

Locock, L. and Boaz, A. (2004) Research, policy and practice – worlds apart?, *Social Policy and Society*, 3(4): 375–84.

Mace, J. (2000) The RAE and university efficiency, *Higher Education Review*, 32(2): 17–36.

MacPherson, Sir W. (1993) *The Stephen Lawrence Inquiry*. London: The Stationery Office.

Mannheim, K. (1968 [originally 1936]) *Ideology and Utopia: An Introduction to the Sociology of Knowledge* (with a Preface by Louis Wirth). London: Routledge and Kegan Paul.

Marchbank, J. and Letherby, G. (2001) Offensive and defensive: feminist pedagogy, student support and higher education, in G. Howie and A. Tauchert (eds) *Gender, Teaching and Research in Higher Education: Challenges for the 21st Century*. London: Ashgate.

Martel, J. (2004) Policing criminological knowledge: the hazards of qualitative research on women in prison, *Theoretical Criminology*, 8(2): 157–89.

Massey, A. and Pyper, R. (2005) *Public Management and Modernisation in Britain*. Basingstoke: Macmillan.

May, T. (1997) *Social Research: Issues, Methods and Process*. Maidenhead: Open University Press.

Mayall, B. (2002) *Towards a Sociology of Childhood: Thinking from Children's Lives*. Buckingham: Open University Press.

Mayall, B., Hood, S. and Oliver, S. (1999) Introduction, in S. Hood, B. Mayall and S. Oliver (eds) (1999) *Critical Issues in Social Research*. Buckingham: Open University Press.

Maynard, M. (1994) Methods, practice and epistemology: the debate about feminism and research, in M. Maynard and J. Purvis (eds) *Researching Women's Lives from a Feminist Perspective*. London: Taylor and Francis.

Maynard, M. K. and Purvis, J. (eds) (1994) *Researching Women's Lives from a Feminist Perspective*. London: Taylor and Francis.

Mears, R. (2001) Called to account: the last autonomous profession, in E. Harrison and R. Mears (eds) *Assessing Sociologists in Higher Education*. Aldershot: Ashgate.

Millen, D. (1997) Some methodological and epistemological issues raised by doing feminist research on non-feminist women, *Sociological Research Online*, 2(3), www.socresonline.org.uk/socresonline/2/3/3.html.

Milligan, C., Bingley, A. and Gatrell, T. (2003) *Cultivating Health and Mental Well-being among Older People in Northern England: End of Project Report*. Lancaster: University of Lancaster.

Mills, C. W. (1959) *The Sociological Imagination*. London: Penguin.

Monnier, E. (1997) Vertical partnerships: the opportunities and constraints which they pose for high quality evaluations, *Evaluation*, 3(1): 110–17.

Morley, L. (1995) Measuring the muse: feminism, creativity and career development in higher education, in L. Morley and V. Walsh (eds) *Feminist Academics: Creative Agents for Change*. London: Taylor and Francis.

Morley, L. (1996) Interrogating patriarchy: the challenges of feminist research, in L. Morley and V. Walsh (eds) *Breaking Boundaries: Women in Higher Education*. London: Taylor and Francis.

Morley, L. (2003) *Quality and Power in Higher Education*. Buckingham: Society for Research into Higher Education and Open University Press.

Morley, L. (2005) Gender equity in Commonwealth higher education, *Women's Studies International Forum*, 28(2/3): 209–21.

Morley, L. and Walsh, V. (eds) (1995) *Feminist Academics: Creative Agents for Change*. London: Taylor and Francis.

National Statistics (2006) Report: conceptions in England and Wales 2004, *Health Statistics Quarterly*, Spring: 55–8.

NHS CRD (NHS Centre for Reviews and Dissemination) (1999) Getting evidence into practice, *Effective Health Care*, 5(1): 1–16.

Noffke, S. and Somekh, B. (2005) Action research, in B. Somekh and C. Lewin (eds) *Research Methods in the Social Sciences*. London: Sage Publications.

Nutley, S. (2003) *Bridging the Policy/Research Divide. Reflections and Lessons from the UK*. St. Andrews: Research Unit for Research Utilisation, University of St. Andrews.

Nutley, S., Davies, H. and Walter, I. (2002) *Evidence Based Policy and Practice: Cross Sector Lessons from the UK*. St. Andrews: Research Unit for Research Utilisation, University of St. Andrews.

Oakley, A. (1981) Interviewing women: a contradiction in terms?, in H. Roberts (ed.) *Doing Feminist Research*. London: Routledge.

Oakley, A. (1999) People's ways of knowing: gender and methodology, in S. Hood, B. Mayall and S. Oliver (eds) *Critical Issues in Social Research*. Buckingham: Open University.

Oakley, A. (2004) Response to 'Quoting and counting: an autobiographical response to Oakley', *Sociology*, 38(1): 191–2.

Okley, J. (1992) Anthropology and autobiography: participatory experience and embodied knowledge, in J. Okley and H. Callaway (eds) *Anthropology and Autobiography*. London: Routledge.

Open Society Institute (2005) *Open Access Publishing and Scholarly Societies*. New York: Open Society Institute.

Osborn, A. and Willcocks, D. (1990) Making research useful and usable, in S. Peace (ed.) *Researching Social Gerontology. Concepts, Methods, and Issues*. London: Sage Publications.

Packwood, A. (2002) Evidence-based policy: rhetoric and reality, *Social Policy and Society*, 1(3): 267–72.

Phoenix, A. (1991) Mothers under twenty: outsider and insider views, in A. Phoenix, A. Woollett and E. Lloyd (eds) *Motherhood: Meanings, Practices and Ideologies*. London: Sage Publications.

Pitcairn, K. (1994) Exploring ways of giving a voice to people with learning disabilities, in B. Humphreys and C. Truman (eds) *Rethinking Social Research*. Aldershot: Avebury.

Punch, M. (1986) *The Politics and Ethics of Fieldwork*. Newbury Park, CA: Sage Publications.

Qureshi, H. (2004) Evidence in policy and practice. What kinds of research designs?, *Journal of Social Work*, 4(1): 7–23.

Raddon, A. (2001) *Research Dissemination in Education: A Literature Review*. Coventry: Department of Continuing Education, University of Warwick.

Ramsay, K. (1996) Emotional labour and organisational research: how I learned not to laugh or cry in the field, in E. Stina Lyon and Joan Busfield (eds) *Methodological Imaginations*. London: Macmillan.

Reid, K., Letherby, G., Mason, L., Burke, E., Taylor, C. and Gough, A. (2005) *Research on Lifelong Learning for Pregnant Young Women and Young Parents in Sandwell*. Coventry: JCJ Solutions and Centre for Social Justice, Coventry University.

Reimer, M. (2004) Does my university contain a woman's voice?, in M. Reimer (ed.) *Inside Corporate U: Women in the Academy Speak Out*. Toronto: Sumach Press.

Reinharz, S. (1983) Experiential research: a contribution to feminist theory, in G. Bowles and R. Klein (eds) *Theories of Women's Studies*. London: Routledge.

Ribbens, J. and Edwards, R. (eds) (1998) *Feminist Dilemmas in Qualitative Research*. London: Sage Publications.

Ritchie, J. and Lewis, J. (eds) (2003) *Qualitative Research Practice*. London: Sage Publications.

Ritchie, J. and Spencer, L. (1994) Qualitative data analysis for applied policy research, in A. Bryman and R. G. Burgess (eds) *Analyzing Qualitative Data*. London: Routledge.

Roberts, H. (1984) Putting the show on the road: the dissemination of research findings, in C. Bell and H. Roberts (eds) *Social Researching, Politics, Problems, Practice*. London: Routledge and Kegan Paul.

Robertson, D. and Dearling, A. (2004) *A Practical Guide to Social Welfare Research*. Lyme Regis: Russell House Press.

Rosenstein, B. (2002) Video use in social science research and programme evaluation, *International Journal of Qualitative Methods*, 1(3): 1–38.

Rossi, P. and Freeman, H. (1993) *Evaluation: A Systematic Approach*. Newbury Park, CA: Sage Publications.

Rossiter, A., Prilleltensky, I. and Walsh-Bowers, R. (2000) A postmodern perspective on professional ethics, in B. Fawcett, B. Featherstone, J. Fook and A. Rossiter (eds) *Practice and Research in Social Work*. London and New York: Routledge.

Royal Liverpool Children's Inquiry (2000) *Royal Liverpool Children's Inquiry Report*. London: House of Commons.

Royle, J., Steel, R., Hanley, B. and Bradburn, J. (2001) *Getting Involved in Research: A Guide for Consumers*. Winchester: Consumers in NHS Research Support Unit.

Sanz-Menendez, L., Bordons, M. and Zuletta, M. Angeles (2001) *Interdisciplinarity as a Multidimensional Concept: Its Measure in Three Different Research Areas*. Unidad de Políticas Comparadas (CSIC) Working Paper 01–04.

Scarman, Lord (1981) *The Brixton Disorders 10–12 April 1981. Report of an Inquiry by the Right Honorable the Lord Scarman, OBE*. Harmondsworth: Penguin.

Scott, A., Skea, J., Robinson, J. and Shove, E. (1999) *Designing 'Interactive' Environmental Research for Wider Social Relevance*. Special Briefing No. 4, ESRC Global Environmental Change Programme.

Scott, J. (2005) Sociology and its others: reflections on disciplinary specialisation and fragmentation, *Sociological Research Online*, 7(2), www.socresonline.org.uk/10/1/scott.html.

SEU (Social Exclusion Unit) (1999) *Teenage Pregnancy*, Cm. 4342. London: The Stationery Office.

Shanley, C., Lodge, M. and Mattick, R. (1996) Dissemination of research findings to alcohol and other drug practitioners, *Drug and Alcohol Review*, 15(1): 89–94.

Sharp, C. (2005) *The Improvement of Public Sector Delivery: Supporting Evidence Based Practice Through Action Research*. Knowledge Transfer Research Findings 2. Edinburgh: The Scottish Executive.

Silverman, D. (1999) *Doing Qualitative Research*. London: Sage Publications.

Smith, A. and Thelwall, M. (2002) Web Impact Factors for Australasian Universities, *Scientometrics*, 54(1–2): 363–80.

Social Science and Humanities Research Council (2005) *About SSHRC*, www.sshrc-crsh.gc.ca/. Accessed November 2005.

Solesbury, W. (2001) *Evidence Based Policy: Whence It Came and Where It's Going*. London: ESRC Centre for Evidence Based Policy and Practice, Queen Mary, University of London.

Somekh, B. and Lewin, C. (eds) (2005) *Research Methods in the Social Sciences*. London: Sage Publications.

Somekh, B., Stronach, I., Lewin, C., Nolan, M. and Stake, J. E. (2005) Participating in the research community, in B. Somekh and C. Lewin (eds) *Research Methods in the Social Sciences*. London: Sage Publications.

Sparkes, A. (1998) Reciprocity in critical research? Some unsettling thoughts, in G. Shacklock and J. Smyth (eds) *Being Reflexive in Critical and Social Educational Research*. London: Falmer.

Spencer, L., Ritchie, J., Lewis, J. and Dillon, L. (2003) *Assessing Quality in Qualitative Evaluation*. London: The Cabinet Office.

Spender, D. (1981) *Man-Made Language*. London: Routledge and Kegan Paul.

Stacey, J. (1991) Can there be a feminist ethnography?, in S. Gluck and D. Patai (eds) *Women's Words, Women's Words, Women's Words: The Feminist Practice of Oral History*. New York: Routledge.

Standing, K. (1998) Writing the voices for the less powerful: research on lone mothers, in J. Ribbens and R. Edwards (eds) *Feminist Dilemmas in Qualitative Research*. London: Sage Publications.

Stanley, L. (1984) How the social science research process discriminates against women, in S. Acker and D. Warren Piper (eds) *Is Higher Education Fair to Women?* London: Routledge.

Stanley, L. (1991) Feminist auto/biography and feminist epistemology, in J. Aaron and S. Walby (eds) *Out of the Margins: Women's Studies in the Nineties*. London: Falmer.

Stanley, L. (1993) On auto/biography in sociology, *Sociology*, 27(1): 41–52.

Stanley, L. (2005) A child of its time: hybrid perspectives on othering in sociology, *Sociological Research Online*, 10(3), www.socresonline.org.uk/10/3.

Stanley, L. and Wise, S. (1983) *Breaking Out: Feminist Consciousness and Feminist Research*. London: Routledge and Kegan Paul.

Stanley, L. and Wise, S. (1990) Method, methodology and epistemology in feminist research processes, in L. Stanley (ed.) *Feminist Praxis: Research, Theory and Epistemology*. London: Routledge.

Stanley, L. and Wise, S. (1993) *Breaking Out Again: Feminist Ontology and Epistemology*. London: Routledge.

Stanley, L. and Wise, S. (2006) Putting it into practice: using feminist fractured foundationalism in researching children in the concentration camps of the South African War, *Sociological Research Online*, 11(1), www.socresonline.org.uk/11/1/stanley.

Steier, F. (ed.) (1991) *Research and Reflexivity*. London: Sage Publications.

Strauss, A. and Corbin, J. (1990) *Basics of Qualitative Research*. London: Sage Publications.

Teenage Pregnancy Unit, Royal College of Midwives and Department of Health (2004) *Teenage Pregnancy: Who Cares?* London: Teenage Pregnancy Unit, Department of Health.

Temple, B. (1997) 'Collegiate accountability' and bias: the solution to the problem?, *Sociological Research Online*, 2(4), www.socresonline.org.uk/socresonline/2/4/8html.

Terre Blanche, M. and Durrheim, K. (eds) (1999) *Research In Practice*. Cape Town: University of Cape Town Press.

Thomas, N. and O'Kane, C. (1999) The ethics of participatory research with children, *Children and Society*, 12(5): 336–48.

Thomas, P. (1998) Is labour just a pain?, *AIMS Journal*, 10(1), www.aims.org.uk/Journal/Vol10No1/labourJustAPain.htm.

Tisdall, K. (2005) Participation or protection? Children, young people and dissemination, in N. Hallowell, J. Lawton and S. Gregory (eds) *Reflections on Research*. Buckingham: Open University Press.

Todhunter, C. (2004) Undertaking action research: negotiating the road ahead, *Social Research Update*, 34. Guildford: University of Surrey.

Trowler, P. (1998) *Academics Responding to Change: New Higher Education Frameworks and Academic Cultures*. Buckingham: Open University and Society for Research into Higher Education.

Truman, C. (2003) Ethics and the ruling relations of research, *Sociological Research Online*, 8(1), www.socresonline.org.uk/8/1/truman.

Tudiver, N. (1999) *Universities for Sale: Resisting Corporate Control over Canadian Higher Education*. Toronto: James Lorimer.

Turner, M. and Beresford, P. (2005) *User Controlled Research. Its Meanings and Potential*. London: Shaping Our Lives and the Centre for Citizenship Participation, Brunel University.

Vaitilingam, R. (2001) *Developing a Media Strategy*. Swindon: ESRC.

Walshe, K. and Rundall, T. (2001) Evidence-based management: from theory to practice in health care, *The Millbank Quarterly*, 79(3): 429–57.

Walter, I., Nutley, S. and Davies, H. (2003) *Research Impact: A Cross Sector Review Literature Review*. St. Andrews: Research Unit for Research Utilisation, University of St. Andrews.

Walter, I., Nutley, S., Percy-Smith, J., McNeish, D. and Frost, S. (2004a) *Improving the Use of Research in Social Care Practice*. Social Care Institute for Excellence Knowledge Review 7. Bristol: The Policy Press.

Walter, I., Nutley, S., Percy-Smith, J., McNeish, D. and Frost, S. (2004b) *Research Utilization and the Social Care Workforce*. St. Andrews: Research Unit for Research Utilisation.

Weaver, J. J. (2000) Childbirth, in J. Ussher (ed.) *Women's Health: Contemporary International Perspectives*. Leicester: British Psychological Society Books.

Webb, S. A. (2001) Some considerations on the validity of evidence-based practice in social work, *British Journal of Social Work*, 31(1): 57–80.

Weiss, C. H. (2000) Which links in which theories shall we evaluate?, in P. Rogers, T. Hacsi, A. Petrosino and T. Huebner (eds) *Program Theory in Evaluation Challenges and Opportunities: New Directions in Evaluation*, No. 87. San Francisco, CA: Jossey-Bass.

White, C., Woodfield, K. and Ritchie, J. (2003) Reporting and presenting data, in J. Ritchie and J. Lewis (eds) *Qualitative Research Practice*. London: Sage Publications.

Wiles, R., Heath, S. and Crow, G. (2005) *Informed Consent and the Research Process*. Methods Briefing 2. Manchester: ESRC Research Methods Programme.

Wilkins, P. (2000) Collaborative approaches to research, in B. Humphries (ed.) *Research in Social Care and Social Welfare: Issues and Debates for Practice*. London: Jessica Kingsley.

Wilkinson, S. and Kitzinger, C. (eds) (1996) *Representing the Other*. London: Sage Publications.

Williams, M. (2005) Situated objectivity, *Journal for the Theory of Social Behaviour*, 35(1): 99–120.

Wise, S. and Stanley, L. (2003) Review article. Looking back and looking forward: some recent feminist sociology reviewed, *Sociological Research Online*, 8(3), www.socresonline.org.uk/8/8/wise.html.

Wolf, D. L (1996) Situating feminist dilemmas in fieldwork, in D. L. Wolf (ed.) *Feminist Dilemmas in Fieldwork*. Boulder, CO: Westview.

Wolff, K. (ed., trans.) (1950) *The Sociology of Georg Simmel*. Glencoe: Free Press.

Working Group on Ethical Review of Student Research in the NHS (Doyal Committee) (2005) *The Ethical Governance and Regulation of Student Projects: A Proposal*. London: Department of Health, www.dh.gov.uk/assetRoot/04/12/08/98/04120898.pdf.

Index